John Hopkins

The Tangier Diaries 1962-1979

Cadmus Editions
San Francisco

First published by La Table Ronde, Paris, 1995

First English language and American edition published 1998 by:

Cadmus Editions
Post Office Box 126
Tiburon-Belvedere
California 94920
http://www.cadmus-editions.com

Acknowledgements

The Paris Review, Number 139, 1996, where a portion of the diary for 1964 was first published.
London Magazine, 31: 9&10, December 1991/January 1992 where "Looking for Jane Bowles' Grave" was first published.

Hopkins, John L., 1938-
Library of Congress Catalog Card Number 97-68253
ISBN 0-932274-50-1 (trade edition)
ISBN 0-932274-51-X (signed edition)

For my sons, Jonathan, Beau, and Cabell: through this journal you will learn more about what my life was like before you were born than I ever knew about my father's.

Introduction

First of all I ought to describe the combination of circumstances that led me to Tangier and how along the way I acquired the ambition to be a writer.

In the summer of 1959, before my senior year at Princeton, I flew back to New York from a cousin's wedding in Atlanta. I was supposed to meet Tony Pell, my roommate at Princeton, who was going to give me the key to his apartment on Gramercy Park which he was lending me for the summer. I rang the bell, but there was no answer. Pell was absent-minded and had forgotten. There I was at eleven o'clock on a Sunday night with a suitcase and no place to sleep, and the next morning I had to begin work at White, Weld & Co. down on Wall Street.

So I walked around the corner to Pete's Tavern on 18th Street and Irving Place where there was a phone. I was going to call around town to find a place to stay for the night. I was in the phone booth with my address book out when a crazy-looking woman started banging on the door. She was the Mediterranean type, with olive skin and a wild hair-do that stuck out in all directions. She banged on the door so hard that the door opened and she wedged herself inside the phone booth with me.

I said to her, "Can't you wait until I'm finished?"

"I have an urgent call to make," she said in a thick foreign accent.

"So do I," I said. "That's my suitcase there. I've got no place to sleep, and I'm supposed to start a summer job on Wall Street at nine o'clock in the morning."

We got to talking. She was a Greek artist called Chryssa. We moved out of the phone booth to the bar. Chryssa lived around the corner at 889 Broadway. After a few beers she invited me back to her place.

Her loft at the corner of 19th Street and Broadway was one huge room. The ceiling was about twenty feet high. The walls were covered with giant canvasses, and the floor was littered with cans of paint. Chryssa didn't have a bath or shower in her studio, just a big bed in the middle of the room.

The next day I got into Pell's apartment. As Chryssa lived around the corner, we saw a lot of each other that summer. Sometimes she'd drop by the apartment for cocktails. Or, when she was drunk and lonely in the middle of the night, she'd stand out in the street, where I'd hear her above the roar of the air-conditioning screaming, "Adon-*ay*-ees! I need you!"

Chryssa was the first bona fide artist I had ever met. Her dedication to her art was total. Her paints and brushes were right there next to the bed. She got up and started work even before she had had a cup of coffee or brushed her teeth. One morning I lay in her bed watching her paint stark naked. For her, life and art were indivisible; she didn't care how she or her place looked as long as she got her work done.

I was about to turn twenty-one and, like many of my college friends, had no clear idea about what I wanted to do with my life. The previous summer I had toured South America, and I hoped to travel again after Princeton. Now Chryssa's devotion to her art woke in me the desire to throw myself heart and soul into some exciting venture, but I gave little thought to how I was going to achieve this vague aspiration.

I did feel strongly, however, about what I did *not* want to do, and that was to become a businessman or banker. I was determined not to get stuck in the same rut my father had. He had given me only two pieces of advice that I remember, and one of them was, "Don't work on Wall Street, son." He had spent most of his working life on Wall Street but had been neither successful nor happy there.

My life was due for a radical change. I had a very hectic social schedule. Every other night, it seemed, there was some deb party out on Long Island, in Connecticut or New Jersey to go to. I weaved my old Ford convertible back into the city at dawn and turned up at work sleepless and hungover. The mornings I spent hiding behind the sports pages of *The New York Times*, trying to catnap. To revive myself, I went out for three-martini lunches with my cronies, which left me so groggy that I spent half the afternoon dozing in one of the cubicles of the men's room at White, Weld & Co. My brother-in-law, who was a junior partner in the firm, used to come in to relieve himself and ask, "Has anyone seen Hopkins? Hasn't he come back from lunch yet?" And there I was locked in the toilet three feet away, trying to sleep amidst the talk and flushing urinals, with my head resting against the toilet roll.

The agent of change arrived in the form of another Princetonian named Joe McPhillips. A mutual friend brought him around to the apartment. McPhillips had graduated the year before and had just gotten out of the army. I hadn't known him very well at Princeton, but we had several friends in common. He was a member of Cottage Club, where most of the Southerners congregated. An honours student in the English department, he was nicknamed "Rebel" not just because he came from Alabama, but because he kept a Triumph motorcycle hidden in a garage off campus, which he used to ride into New York to see Tennessee Williams' plays. His dynamic personality and intellectual reputation had made him a big man on campus, which was practically unheard of for someone who wasn't a top athlete. He had read Camus, Sartre, Stendhal and Proust, while I played on the ice hockey team, chased girls, ate my meals at the Ivy Club, and studied just enough to keep from getting kicked out.

After a few drinks we hopped into my convertible and drove to Chinatown for supper. The summer of 1959 was one of the hottest on record. New York was like a jungle, with the natives beating drums and walking around half-naked. The kids on the street had opened a fire hydrant and were directing streams of water at passing cars with coffee cans opened at both ends. We got soaking wet, but it felt good.

The tropical heat reminded me of Rio. While we fumbled with chopsticks I told McPhillips about the trip I had taken to South America the summer before. It was the first time I had set foot outside the U.S., and I had kept a diary of my travels.

McPhillips said he had just met a fellow called Ted Achilles whose father was the U.S. Ambassador to Peru. Ted had been visiting Peru, and he told Joe about a beautiful jungle town called Tingo Maria where you could lead an exotic life and make a fortune growing coffee.

I'd heard of Tingo Maria. My uncle had flown for a Peruvian airline after the war. When the airline went bust, he and his wife had panned for gold in the Huallaga River not far from Tingo. He had told me plenty of stories about Peru. At Princeton I'd read *Lost Trails, Lost Cities* by Colonel Percy Fawcett, the English explorer, which whetted my appetite for adventure in South America.

That night we went to an off-Broadway production of *Our Town* by Thornton Wilder. During the show I kept thinking about South America. This coffee-growing venture sounded very romantic to me. It answered my urge to travel and to distance myself from my divorce-torn family. The next day after work I walked up to the Public Library on 5th Avenue and 42nd Street and started reading up on coffee in South America.

Toward the end of August I opened the paper to the sports section and noticed a headline: PERUVIAN COFFEE KING

IN NEW YORK. The article was about a man called Jorge Hartens who was in town to see his protégé Alex Olmedo play in the Davis Cup against Australia.

I got hold of McPhillips who said, "We've got to meet this guy!" I phoned the Waldorf where the article said Mr. Hartens was staying and spoke to the Coffee King himself. I told him that a friend and I were thinking of buying or starting up a coffee plantation in Peru. To my amazement Mr. Hartens sounded very interested in our project and invited us to breakfast the next day at 6AM to talk about it.

We turned up in our business suits and had coffee with the Coffee King. He didn't speak much English, but he was very enthusiastic about growing coffee in Peru. Peruvian coffee wasn't well known in the world, he said, but its quality was just as good as what came out of Colombia. "Boys," he said, "you can do all the research on coffee in New York that you want, but the only way to find out about the coffee situation in Tingo Maria is to come to Peru and see for yourselves. I'm going back after the Davis Cup, and I'll be glad to help you any way I can." He handed us two tickets to Forest Hills and said, "I hope to see you in Lima. You are welcome to stay in my home. *Mi casa es su casa.* I will put my car and my boat at your disposal. My son will take you into the jungle in his jeep and show you coffee plantations."

Joe and I went out the revolving door of the Waldorf in a daze. The generosity of the man had stunned us. We decided then and there, on the sidewalk of Park Avenue with the yellow taxis racing past, to drop everything and go to Peru. The Coffee King was offering his hospitality; it was too good an opportunity to pass up.

The problem for Joe was money. He hadn't been able to save enough from his job at Highway Trailers to buy a bus ticket to Philadelphia, let alone airfare to Lima plus his expenses down there. However, he'd try to borrow the money from friends who were interested in backing our project.

My problem was Princeton. In two weeks I was due back for my senior year.

When I began to get cold feet about the trip, Chryssa had one word of advice: "Go!" And she expounded on the mysteries of pre-Colombian art.

"What are you waiting for?" she said. "This man has appeared from nowhere to help you realize your dreams. How often does that happen in life? It's an omen you shouldn't ignore. Go to Peru or you'll regret it for the rest of your life!"

That did it. A week later Joe and I flew to Lima and checked into the Hotel Bolivar. We called on Ambassador Achilles. He put us in touch with agricultural experts who advised us on the state of the world coffee market and the quality of the Peruvian crop. They produced maps and pointed out the most promising coffee-growing regions. Mr. Hartens received us in his magnificent office and introduced us to his sons and business associates. Within hours a number of shady characters descended like vultures on the Hotel Bolivar. Assuming us to be millionaires, these Peruvians wanted to sell us coffee plantations in the jungle, banana farms on the coast, and cattle-fattening stations up in the Andes—properties, it turned out, they had never visited. We didn't tell them we were just a couple of college kids who had had to borrow money from our families to buy plane tickets to Peru.

What with the language barrier and these dubious hombres pressing us to sign on the dotted line, it all became a bit confusing. To escape we flew over the Andes in a Fawcett Airlines DC-3 to Tingo Maria. The local bank manager met us at the airport and showed us several coffee farms in the area. We drove for hours along jungle tracks, tramped through the rainforest, and listened to reports from farm workers and managers. Each evening we returned to the hotel to find another German or Italian waiting to take us to his *finca*. Everything, it seemed, was for sale; Joe and I were viewed as Yankee benefactors who were going to deliver these impoverished farmers from their lonely lives in the jungle.

We flew back to Lima, and Mr. Hartens' son drove us over the Andes to visit Chanchamayo, another coffee region. We went to a bullfight, surfed in the Pacific, and tramped for miles through the *barriadas* or shantytowns that surrounded the city. The vultures that patrolled the skies over Lima were not, for me, an ominous presence; they came to symbolize the soaring sense of freedom I was beginning to experience in Peru.

We had heard so many pros and cons on the subject of coffee that it was impossible to make a commitment. From our ruminations another course of action emerged. Why not travel around the world? We took the tram to Callao, hired a launch and chugged around the harbour, offering ourselves as deckhands on any ship heading for the Orient. When nothing came of this, we had no choice but to go home, vowing to return to Peru the following year to continue our investigations.

I went back to Princeton for my senior year and managed to graduate. The next summer I spent studying Spanish at the University of Madrid and returned to Peru with Joe in September. Anticipating a longer visit, we rented a room at the Pension Americana on Carabaya off Plaza San Martín. Our circle of acquaintances quickly expanded. We went on an archaeological dig (grave-robbing really) in the north of the country and visited farms and ranches up and down the coast, always returning to Lima, the center. Joe gave English lessons to earn extra cash and I worked hard on my Spanish. McPhillips, the teacher, set me a list of European and American literary classics, beginning with Thomas Mann's *The Magic Mountain*. For the first time in my life I began to read voraciously. I walked all over the city beneath the vultures, feeling free and excited by the possibilities of life in that strange, sad land.

Joe befriended Malcolm Burke, an eccentric Yale man who had lived for many years in Peru. Burke wrote for *The Andean Airmail* and *Peruvian Times* and was working on a biography of Santa Rosa de Lima. When he took his hefty manuscript to New York, his route was typical of the man. He travelled by train to Cerro de Pasco in the Andes, thence by bus to Tingo and Pucallpa, by *vapor* down the Ucayali River to Iquitos, where he boarded a Booth Line freighter bound for the U.S. He loaned us his penthouse apartment in Edificio Jorge Chavez on Avenida Wilson. With it came Olinda, his Indian maid of whom he said, "You may fondle, fuck, or flagellate, but do not pamper."

We pampered her, she quit, and we set off for the interior. Following Burke's overland trail, we spent several weeks on coffee farms in the Tingo area before Joe flew to Tarapoto to investigate cotton and cattle prospects in San Martín province. On the bank of the Huallaga I found two Indians building a balsa raft. They agreed, for a price, to take me with them. For the next week I floated through the jungle like a modern-day Huck Finn, helping my companions avoid whirlpools and navigate *malpasos*. I slept on the river bank and traded beer for food with naked Indians.

Joe and I met again in Tarapoto. Sitting in the village square, we reached a joint conclusion: we were not prepared to spend the rest of our lives in the jungle. Every farmer Joe had met was either losing money or struggling to break even. There was a glut of coffee on the world market. To keep prices from dropping further, Brazil had thrown half its crop into the sea.

Neither was I eager to return with my tail between my legs to the U.S., where my parents would almost certainly pressure me to get a job or go to graduate school. I wanted to see more of the world before settling down. So in that sunny plaza, with the parrots screaming over our heads, we decided to go to Europe. But not before completing our trip down the Amazon as far as Iquitos.

Three months later Joe and I were back in New York boarding the old Italian Line *Saturnia* for Naples. In my pocket I had a letter from a Princetonian called Sam Small, inviting any member of the Ivy Club to visit him on his ranch in Kenya. Elated by what seemed another unique opportunity to travel, I had written him that Joe and I were on our way. Our plan was to stay in Europe for a while, buy a motorcyle and drive it to Kenya.

The trip across the Atlantic was uneventful except for insomnia. Unable to sleep, I studied Italian and started reading *The Remembrance of Things Past*.

Sitting in the Taverna Margutta near the Spanish Steps, where we made our headquarters in Rome, I came across an ad in *The Daily American*: "Reader wanted for blind Englishman." Why not? I rang the number. A polite voice explained that an elderly English writer called Percy Lubbock needed a companion in his villa in Lerici on the Golfo della Spezia. I gave a quick resumé about myself, adding that there were two of us. All the better, the voice said; we could take turns reading.

We took a train to La Spezia and were met at the station by Jocelyn Lubbock. He drove us to Gli Scafari, his uncle's splendid villa overlooking the Mediterranean. Percy was wheeled onto the loggia by his manservant, Mario. We hit it off immediately. Percy had been a friend of Henry James and had Henry James' watch, which was duly produced for our inspection. During lunch, a magnificent feast prepared by Mario's wife, Elena, we described our adventures in Peru. When we were shown our rooms, complete with marble floors, four-poster beds tented with mosquito netting, and unobstructed views of the sea, Joe and I reckoned we had landed in paradise.

Percy, the author of many books, including *Earlham*, *Roman Pictures*, *Portrait of Edith Wharton*, and *The Craft of Fiction*, had worked with E. M. Forster in a Red Cross Hospital in Cairo in 1915 and had known Rupert Brooke. He was a mine of literary gossip and information going back half a century.

Every day at Gli Scafari was more or less the same. Mario would push Percy onto the loggia about eleven, and I would read the Italian and English newspapers to him. (The airmail edition of *The Times* arrived each morning.) After an hour or so Percy would remark,

"Doesn't reading make you thirsty, my boy?"

This was the signal for Mario to roll out the drinks tray. We sipped Italian cocktails until lunch time. When Joe took over reading duty, I dove off the rocks below Percy's villa. We dressed for lunch, the high point of the day. Elena prepared fresh fish (her son was a local fisherman), pasta with vegetables and mountains of fruit.

After lunch came the inevitable siesta. Percy surfaced about four, and Joe or I would read until seven, when drinks were served. If the evenings were fine, we would dine on the loggia. Afterwards one or the other of us would read for another hour.

When we weren't reading we swam. I bought a snorkel, mask and flippers and explored underwater caves up and down the coast. Percy told me to be on the lookout for the "Eton fish," a blue and black denizen that frequented those waters, but I never saw it. I often swam at night, which Percy called "swimming in ink."

Joe read the plays of Tennessee Williams in his southern accent, while I laboured through Lionel Trilling's biography of Matthew Arnold. As our conversations turned more literary, Percy challenged me to spend a day and a night without food or water on a rocky islet just off the promontory below Gli Scafari, making notes of everything I saw, felt, or thought.

It was a challenge I quickly accepted. Having just read Hermann Hesse's *Siddhartha*, I was eager for any sort of ascetic experience. On June 11, 1961, one week after Percy's eighty-second birthday, I swam to the island, pushing ahead of me a rubber raft containing a sleeping bag, cigarettes, pocket knife, flashlight, and notebook and pen to record every detail of my twenty-four hour exile. Percy turned up the gramophone full blast, and Joe announced the evening's menu in a loud voice in a mocking effort to break my resolve and lure me ashore. But I stuck to my rock, scribbling away. I reckon my writing career began that night.

But the purpose of the trip was to keep moving. Sam Small was writing letters from Kenya, describing the wildlife and urging me to join him. Joe and I took the train to Munich where I bought a beautiful white BMW motorcycle, which we christened the "White Nile"(we were reading Alan Moorehead's books on Africa at the time). We whizzed over the Alps, stopping in Lerici to say goodbye. Our departure from Gli Scafari was particularly poignant because we had become genuinely fond of Percy. Old and ailing, he would never leave his villa, and it was clear that our new motorcycle would carry us far away.

We motored south to Naples and took the boat to Tunis, arriving the day the Bizerte crisis erupted. To escape the violence, we headed south to the tranquility of Kairouan and the Grand Sahara. Near the Libyan border, we were surrounded by a band of club-wielding vigilantes. Incensed by French brutality at Bizerte, they probably would have murdered us had we not produced our American passports.

We raced past the frontier post into Libya and were chased by a patrol car for fifty miles across the desert. At a road block at Zuwaran we were stopped by policemen who threw us into jail for entering the country illegally. An Oxford-educated colonel rescued us, insisting we stay for tea (strong, smoky green tea) before letting us go.

From Tripoli we headed east across a landscape trashed by the armies of Rommel and Montgomery. Countless oil drums, burnt-out trucks, armoured cars and tanks littered the desert from horizon to horizon. We sought refuge from this military junkyard in the classical purity of Leptis Magna, Emperor Septimus Severus' city. For a day and a night we wandered in eerie marble silence before pushing on to Cyrene and Apollonia, ancient Greek cities in the Libyan "Alps", where the cool air was a welcome change from the inferno of the desert. Next it was Tobruk and El Alamein with their massive monuments to the war dead.

The sheer intoxication of riding the machine across Libya elicited violent expressions of ecstasy. I screamed my joy into the wind as the magnificent countryside whipped by, the desert and sea stretching toward separate infinities to the right and left.

The White Nile purred on, attracting crowds wherever we went. I was reading *The Alexandria Quartet*, but Durrell's city bore little resemblance to what we found. We reached Cairo in mid-August, having been on the road for six weeks. The 100° heat was grinding us down.

While in Cairo I climbed the Great Pyramid at dawn and, with my Swiss army knife, etched my name into the rock alongside those of Napoleon's soldiers. On to Luxor, a Coptic town seen through the haze of sickness and fatigue. We visited the Valley of Kings by donkey. McPhillips, weakened by fever, took the train to Aswan while I drove the machine. There was no road, and I spent seven hours following a track across the desert in 120° heat. I don't think I would have survived the ordeal had I not brought along a pocketful of lemons. Two blow-outs later

I arrived in Aswan to find McPhillips in the hospital with fever. The German doctor put me into the next bed and treated me for sunstroke.

We caught the Nile steamer for Wadi Halfa and spent two nights travelling third class, sleeping on the deck and cooking our own food. We stopped at Abou Simbel at 3 AM and explored the gigantic temple by moonlight. At Wadi Halfa we boarded the "Desert Express" for an unbearably hot and dusty train trip across the Nubian desert to Khartoum. Unable to sleep, I got down at one of the stops and walked forward to the engine. The engineer and fireman welcomed me aboard, and I spent the rest of the night with them roaring across the desert. The ancient engine, like a powerful but stubborn beast of burden, was kept going by alternatively beating it with huge wrenches and twisting knobs and making fine adjustments. It would not run at a constant speed but went faster and faster until the tracks began to swivel on the sand. An alarm clock hung on a string around the engineer's neck; rocks in the desert and the occasional mud hut told him where he was.

I could neither hear nor speak for the clamour of the machine. When I climbed down at dawn, grimy with grease and coal dust, and staggered back to my dusty railroad car, I felt I'd been to hell or heaven, I didn't know which.

A few hours after arriving in Khartoum I was shaking hands with the Prime Minister of the Sudan at a polo match. Our host, Col. Hilary Hook, found us quarters at the university. When our fevers subsided, we took the train to Kosti and boarded the *Marra*, an old stern wheeler that was to be our home for the next two weeks.

To relieve the tedium of travelling across the Sudd, a swamp as big as the British Isles, I worked on my diary. By putting down on paper thoughts about the books I was reading and descriptions of what I'd seen and done, I was able to give form to the formless life we were leading.

Writing reassured me; it provided me with a daily mission; it gave me confidence in a strange land. My notebook became a friend that I looked forward to communing with every day.

We landed in Juba and once more boarded the faithful White Nile. In British East Africa began a series of misadventures that were to colour the rest of our trip. The road to Uganda was a quagmire. We were almost killed by a white man who raced past us in a Land Rover, sliding all over the road and spattering us with mud. We ran into the same drunken individual in a bar in Gulu and got into a fight. The next morning, nursing sore knuckles and various bruises, we set off for Murchison Falls Game Park.

We entered the reserve on a deeply rutted road. The White Nile kept keeling over, but I was more worried by buffalo and lion tracks. Tall grass hemmed us in on both sides. I couldn't see the animals, but I could smell them and expected one to show itself in a disagreeable manner any minute. After eight miles we reached the official entrance to the reserve to be informed that motorcycles were not allowed in.

I soon learned the reason why. Setting off at our own risk, we were surrounded by a herd of buffalo. They paid us no attention, but we felt extremely vulnerable pushing the motorcycle among them. The track became almost impassable. Following heavy rains, the mud was a foot deep. The White Nile must have gone over a dozen times that day but never stopped running. It took us four hours to cover twenty miles to the lodge at Paroa. After washing the mud off myself, I drove the White Nile into the shower and scrubbed her until she was white and shiny. That night in the restaurant the white hunter approached us and, in a drunken and aggressive manner, informed us that we had entered the park illegally and had to leave the next day.

We crossed the Nile and headed through the southern half of the park which contained some 14,000 elephant. It wasn't long before we got into a fix.

Cresting a rise, we found a lone elephant blocking the road ahead of us. We stopped and waited for him to move, but he started walking toward us, ears flapping. We were about to beat a retreat when another elephant stepped from the bush onto the road behind us. There wasn't a tree in sight, only elephants—long lines of them, tails in trunks, strolling peacefully like Babar and his friends, but these two rogues looked as though they wanted to squeeze us like bookends.

When the first elephant moved to the edge of the track, we decided to make a dash past him. To our horror the White Nile suddenly conked out. There was one frozen moment beside a great gray wall that we could have reached out and touched. Incredibly, he ignored us. The White Nile roared to life and we bolted away.

The motorcycle finally gave up the ghost in Nairobi. Leaving her in the care of an Indian mechanic, we were whisked off in a chauffeur-driven car to Impala Ranch. Sam was not at home. A china bowl on the dining-room table contained a small mountain of letters. We were absorbed in reading our first mail in three months when Sam walked in and commented petulantly,

"That's more mail than I've gotten in ten years."

That night we reminisced about Princeton and the Ivy Club. As Sam's guns had been confiscated, my door was guarded by a Kikuyu tribesman with a bow and poison arrows. Breakfast was served at 5 AM, when Sam announced that his "boys" had informed him that there was to be a big raid by Somali cattle rustlers. We would have to alert the neighbours, drive the cattle in, make a fort, and fight for our lives.

By now I realized that our host was not only alcoholic but

paranoid; yet we were uncertain how to react to this announcement. A few hours later we found him sprawled unconscious in bed, an empty bottle of gin beside him. After that he locked himself in the creamery. We never saw him again.

For two weeks we were marooned on Impala Ranch. The Land Rover was up on blocks, and the car battery was dead. But we had plenty of food and drink, staff to wait on us and miles of country to explore. We rode around the ranch on Sam's horses and chased the reticulated giraffes through the thorn trees. Sam owned forty dogs, ranging from Yorkshire terriers to Rhodesian Ridgebacks. One evening as we were sitting on the verandah, admiring the view of Mt. Kenya, a baboon migration passed near the house. Hundreds of baboons, some with babies sitting on their backs, were moving peacefully from one rock outcropping to another, when Sam's dogs charged. A ferocious battle out of pre-history ensued; several dogs were killed, while others came back dragging their guts and had to be destroyed.

We were eventually rescued from our island in the veldt, but things went from bad to worse. Joe came down with pneumonia. My binoculars were stolen, and the suitcase Joe had airmailed from Khartoum never arrived. The White Nile, despite a new motor sent free of charge from the BMW factory in Munich, was still not running the way she used to. We hitchhiked to Mombasa, hoping to catch a boat to Bombay or Jakarta. When that failed, we flew to Paris. The ailing motorcycle followed in a wooden crate.

As funds were low, Joe started teaching English at a French lycée near Versailles. Answering an ad in the *Herald Tribune*, I got a job running a school for the U.S. Army at Etain in eastern France. I lived at 5, rue du Pont with Mme. Xardel, a widow who had seen the Germans of two world wars tramp past her door. Joe and I met in Paris on weekends. Agonizing over what to do next, we talked half-heartedly of going back to South America. Our families, meanwhile, were predictably urging us to return to the U.S.

Every morning I went off to Caserne Sidi Brahim to teach fifty-year-old sergeants how to read and write. In my spare time I wandered the trenches that scarred the battlefields around Verdun. It was a lonely, unsatisfactory existence. After Africa and South America, Europe was too cold, too tame, too civilized. My only consolation was my diary. Inspired by Gide's *Journals*, I had begun to note my determination to become a writer. But of what? Essays, novels, short stories? I had no idea.

In Paris Joe had run into Pauline Pinto from Birmingham, Alabama. Her brother, J.T., had been his best friend at Princeton. Pauline and her husband, Joe, were living in a beautiful apartment at 59, Boulevard Lannes. Joe Pinto had gone to Lawrenceville and Yale, but he came from a Moroccan Jewish family and had grown up in Tangier. He talked a lot about Morocco. If we missed Africa so much, he asked, why didn't we go to Tangier?

The idea was appealing, but what would we do when we got there? we wondered. How were we going to support ourselves in Morocco? The answer, like Jorge Hartens' name in the sports section of *The New York Times*, appeared out of thin air. Joe Pinto's father had been one of the founders of The American School of Tangier. We wrote the school and filled out forms. Our teaching experience in Peru and France came in handy. The Pintos recommended us, and we were given jobs in Morocco! On July 2, 1962, we hopped on the White Nile and, for the second time in a year, set off for Africa.

1962

July 12 - Hotel Olid, Calle Cristianos, Tangier

Arrived last night via the *Mons Calpe* ferry from Gibraltar. The first person we ran into was Frank Wisner,[1] washing his feet in a fountain outside the old Spanish post office. He's been sent here by the U.S. State Dept. to learn Arabic. We sat at the Café Central in the Zoco Chico until 4AM, drinking Fundador and reminiscing about Princeton. The urchins wouldn't let us alone. Do these diminutive hustlers ever sleep? Do they have parents who wonder where they are? The Zoco Chico, apparently, is the square that inspired Tennessee Williams to write *Camino Real*. According to Wisner, the master is in Tangier right now.

July 14 - La Place de la Kasbah

We parked the motorcycle by a high white wall with pink geraniums spilling down. A Moroccan kid pointed at a green door: "Englishman live there!" We knocked, and a man dressed in impeccable tweeds opened and welcomed us inside.

We entered a courtyard paved with green and red tiles. White Moorish arches ran along one side. A gnarled old fig tree, whose branches were so heavy they had to be supported by chains—the chains themselves had long ago become embedded in the wood—shaded the patio with its broad leafy expanse. This was the tree, our host explained, where Samuel Pepys wrote his Tangier diary back in 1683, when England ruled this city. Green figs as big

1. Friend of Hopkins and McPhillips at Princeton University.

as your fist hung precariously over our heads.

A bust of Seneca scowled from the top of a Roman column. Water splashed in a little fountain. A yellow-crested cockatoo hung upside down in a cage, shrieking, "*¡Patatas fritas! ¡Patatas fritas!*" Somewhere someone was moaning an old Andalusian lament. The scene was Mediterranean and timeless. It could have been a house in ancient Rome or Greece, Leptis Magna or Alexandria.

This was the home of Jim Wyllie, artist and long-time resident of Tangier. We told him we'd come to Tangier to teach at the American School and wanted to live in the Kasbah. No sooner said than done. He led us along a whitewashed alley to another carved and studded keyhole door belonging to a tiny house built into the Kasbah wall. It was for rent and we could have it!

July 17

Wisner has been in Tangier only two weeks but seems to know everybody. Today he took us to visit Paul Bowles in his apartment behind the American Consulate. We sat respectfully on the floor while the man of letters made tea. Bowles was dressed conservatively in coat and tie, like a university professor. You come to North Africa in the middle of summer and everyone is wearing tweeds!

I said I'd come to teach at the American School but wanted to write a novel. Bowles nodded non-committally: he'd heard that one before. Jane Bowles hobbled in. She radiated a kind of twisted, broken beauty. She wanted to see what the American boys looked like. Her welcoming smile conveyed a wound. She left with the words, "Remember, Fluffy, Tennessee is coming for dinner!"

July 22

Saw T. Williams at Sun Beach today. Not an impressive sight in a bathing suit with a rather large pot belly and greyish skin. He seemed to be in a rush—always going somewhere in a hurry, never stopping or taking his time. Arab boys danced about him like bright leaves fluttering from an ageing tree. The bodies of the poor: lean, sculpted, brown, with every muscle showing; the bodies of the rich: white, flabby, shapeless, ugly.

July 31

Now alone and approaching my 24th birthday. I wonder what will become of me. Where shall I go and what will I do? Who will come into my life and who will leave it? Who will be touched and who will reach out to me?

August 2

Forty-five pages of my novel written in nameless dedication.

August 6

Birthday yesterday; today 24.

August 28

At an art show at the Casino de Tanger yesterday an American woman came up and introduced herself. A black sheath dress, bright red lipstick and piercing hazel eyes. Thirty-three years old, she has lived in Tangier five years and teaches at the American School. Carla Grissmann by name. With her hair done up in a bun, she does look a bit like a school marm—a very chic Parisian school marm.

September 5 - 62 Bab el Assa, Place de la Kasbah, Tangier

This diminutive Moorish house is built into the old stone rampart of the Kasbah. Three storeys straight up, immaculately whitewashed with red tile floors. First floor: dining room, kitchen and breakfast nook; second floor: two bedrooms and bath; top floor: living room and terrace. From the table where I work I have a panoramic view over the sprawling medina, across the Bay of Tangier and the Strait to the Spanish coast as far as Jebel Tariq (Gibraltar) and Jebel Musa (Mount Moses)—the Pillars of Hercules.

When I take a break from writing, I step out onto the terrace to smoke a cigarette and watch the ships slide through the Strait toward exotic and unknown ports. The hubbub of Moroccan life rises from the city below me. I inhale the mingling scents of wisteria, ripe figs and cook smoke from grilling kebabs. I am stunned by the beauty of the setting, and by my good fortune to have stumbled into it.

September 7

Tangier characters: Sonia and Narayan Kamalakar. He's an Indian prince and she, apparently, is descended from a noble Georgian family. He resembles a rather limp beanpole, while she's shaped like a rubber ball. Then there's Tamara, Sonia's daughter, 19 years old with a mane of auburn hair. They all squeeze into Villa Darna, a tiny house on a track fenced in by live cane off rue d'Ecosse, at the bottom of the Old Mountain. Poor as church mice, they manage nonetheless to maintain a spiritual identity. Once a week there's a poetry reading at Villa Darna (Arabic: Our House). The arrogant and learned Alan Ansen[1] read from his former employer, W. H. Auden. We sat on stones in the garden.

September 12

This evening I was having a beer at the Café de Paris when a line of camels, ridden by lean, hawklike men in black turbans and blue robes, ambled by.

"¡Vamos a la Kasbah!" they called in sibilant desert voices. Meaning: they had been invited (paid) to form part of the decor for Barbara Hutton's annual blast in the

1. American poet and former amanuensis to W. H. Auden, he helped William Burroughs assemble the manuscript of *The Naked Lunch*.

Kasbah.[1] Later we eavesdropped on a pair of French queens dolling themselves up for the big event in the house across the street (the alley we live on is so narrow I can practically reach across and tap on my neighbour's window). Eyeshadow, make-up, squeals of excitement punctuated by murderous asides.

September 14

The Kasbah gate has been widened so BH's great green Rolls Royce can glide through. When the alley narrows and the monster can proceed no farther without wedging itself between converging walls, the chauffeur hops out—a blond uniformed giant of the stormtrooper ilk—picks up the heiress—legs swinging limply like a rag doll's—and carries her the last few steps to her palace in the Kasbah.

October 13

As the American School keeps Spanish hours, Joe, Carla and I lunch in a restaurant on the beach. The summer season is over, and the tourists have departed. The Moroccan waiter set up a table for us on the sand. Soccer games ebb and flow across the wide beach. The shouts of the young players, as they struggled for the ball, were echoed by the hungry mewing of seagulls that wheeled above our heads.

For Carla, food is a way of life. I have never known a woman who loves food so much but, mysteriously, she stays slim. Grilled sardines, Moroccan salad, and a bottle of wine. After lunch she put on a black terry-cloth bikini, and we waded out through the soft lapping waves of the bay and fell into the water. These clear October days the Strait is like a mirror. Distant fishing boats dot the surface like flies on a window pane.

1. Sidi Hosni, the moorish house Barbara Hutton bought from the American diplomatic agent Maxwell Blake in 1946, where she gave her exotic parties.

October 15

Today Mina came to cook. Petite, ivory-skinned, dark eyes, wrapped and veiled in white, Spanish speaking. Our first lunch: *œufs mayonnaise* with the hard-boiled yolks removed (replaced by rolled anchovies) and crumbled over the mayo; San Pedro (John Dory *en anglais*) and a miraculous salad. We pay her 5 dirhams (about a dollar) a day to clean and cook, and everybody is happy.

October 25

Since the weather changed asthma is nearly killing me in this place. I feel weak, enervated, the strength dragged out of me. It has been raining for days, and the walls of our house have turned green with mold. Apparently the sand from which the cement is made comes straight from the beach full of salt, which of course absorbs and retains moisture. The sheets never dry out. Awake since 4AM, it was four hours before I had the energy to get out of bed. Thus a part of the morning—in which I had planned a great deal of writing—ruined.

November 11

During the winter, everyone in Tangier suffers from the damp. Central heating doesn't exist. The other day I overheard an Englishman in a café telling a visitor how he heated his house. His solution is to take a can of gasoline home every night. He pours a little into a pot on the floor in the middle of the room and throws a match at it. Whoomp!—a big cloud of flame and hot air shoots up. It took the chill off the room, but every fifteen minutes or so he had to do it again. Whoomp! Whoomp!—that's how one man passes the winter evenings in Tangier, finally tucking himself into a bed sandbagged with hot water bottles.

November 15

The school, it wears me out. My students—Moroccan, Spanish, American, French and English; Muslim, Christian, Hindu and Jew—they take too much from me. I love teaching but wish I were digging ditches instead. At the end of the day nothing is left. Too tired to write.

December 1

A crystal day inspired Joe and me to visit Tetuan, a snow white town spilling down the rocky hillside. We bounced through cactus country in a native bus that stopped every mile or so to let off a robed patriarch with turban and stick, or to take aboard pretty, clear-skinned Anjera girls with their bundles and babies. No hurry or rush. I was reminded of our archaeological expedition to the Valle de las Culebras in Peru, and the bus trip over the Andes from Cerro de Pasco to Huanuco.

December 7

A talk at the school by Carlton Coon, Harvard anthropologist. He has been attempting to trace Berber origins in the Rif Mountains. The Vandals, a German tribe, passed through Morocco (429 - 435AD) on their way to Carthage, leaving behind a trail of mysterious blue eyes.

December 8

Another asthma attack has landed me in the Italian Hospital. Carla brought soup to revive me.

December 9

What am I expecting? Love, I suppose, from all directions. Joe reads this and laughs.

December 15

Carla's way of making soup: Go to market and buy the

oldest and toughest bird she can find. She takes it to the chicken killer and waits, eyes averted, while he chops off the head, feathers and guts this mother of roosters. She boils the bird all day before fishing the carcass out of the pot and giving it to the cat. She arrives in the Kasbah carrying the pot wrapped Moroccan-style in a *hammam* towel to keep it warm. Her high heels slip on the Kasbah cobbles, her ankles are at all angles, and her long legs wobble.

December 19

Lunch in the Kasbah with Jane Bowles who, by her interest and intensity, drew me out of my shell. I found myself talking passionately about family matters that ordinarily I would consider of minor interest to others: i.e. my unhappy sister, my parents, their divorce and its crippling effect upon all of us. When she left, Jane hugged me and said, "There is no minor and no major." She radiates a skewed beauty, as reflected in the cracked pocket mirror she carries in her purse.

December 23 - Whitehouse, N.J.

In my mother's house. I almost said "home," but that no longer applies. Tangier is my home now.

4AM. Insomniac, unable to sleep, I stare at these team photographs that my mother has had framed and hung on the walls. Two years ago I was playing ice hockey for Princeton. Today I am living in a North African seaport attempting to write my first novel. My life has changed out of all recognition. Peru started the process; Tangier is continuing it.

December 24, 10.05 PM

Christmas Eve and I am exhausted. The last twenty-four hours have been a newsreel sequence of faces hurtling by, old friends and acquaintances, each summoning up a segment of my past that now seems irrelevant.

Heard for the first time the voice of Joan Baez. I thought I was falling in love, not with her but with an image of beauty (undefined) she aroused within me.

December 25, 10 PM

The giving of so many gifts to the point that they become valueless. One is lost in a sea of affluence in which material possessions accumulate and crowd one out of the house. One has money and simply buys whatever is pleasing, as many or as much as one wants. This is a society in which every material desire is immediately fulfilled. The most beautiful and expensive gifts are thrown together with countless stocking-fillers. Having lived austerely for the past two years, I am now repelled by all this.

December 27 - New York

Saw *Who's Afraid of Virginia Woolf* last night. Words that get under the skin and expose the soul. The Greeks did it and so did Dostoevsky.

1963

January 1 - New York

A new year begun on a day like all others, cold and blustery.
   Saw Genet's *The Blacks* last night. The reaction of the audience was as riveting as the play, with white people looking worried and black people clapping and cheering when the black actors screamed out their fury over the injustices done to them by the white race.

January 3

X-rays reveal two cracked vertebrae in my back. Probably from that motorcycle accident in Spain last summer.

January 7 - Tangier

Home and happy! But it's hard work teaching school all day and trying to write at night. I go to the wine bottle for inspiration, but it doesn't work. I accomplish more on Saturday and Sunday mornings, when the mind is fresh.

January 11

What is it about Tangier that produces such euphoria? Is it because the writing went well today?

March 11

Haven't written anything in this notebook lately, *but* . . . the novel *Christopher* is finished.

March 17

Sylvia Plath dead in London. I know what killed her: this

awful winter. It almost killed me. Bad enough here in Morocco—God knows what the weather was like in England.

March 23

Saturday. With the book done, I have come to hate weekends. The weekdays are busy—filled by my job at the American School, but the weekend has become a vacuum. This morning started cloudy and cold. I mailed some letters and returned to the house brimming with nervousness and unused energy. Now that the book is finished I have nothing. At 11AM I went to sleep again. Awoke frustrated and cold. Corrected papers. By lunch I was nearly out of my mind with frustration. Rode the White Nile (90MPH) to the Forêt Diplomatique. Then drove the machine onto the Atlantic beach, which was as hard and as flat as a tennis court. For miles I rode, my happiness bursting like the waves. Seagulls followed, skimming low among the breakers. The flatness of the beach, the purr of the BMW and limitless space confirmed that my powers of creativity are unlimited, that I can and will write. I *can* find inspiration anywhere, any time.

Later, back in Tangier, drinking Fundador at Bar Montero, I felt possessed by some fantastic devil-spirit. Moroccans passing in the street looked at me as if I was a little mad. We laughed together over these mutual unspoken confidences.

March 30

A Saturday so blue. A sky and sea to defy Matisse. Their message is too complete, too strong to interpret. Suddenly, it's hot. I'll go swimming in the sea for the first time this year. A big event.

March 31

What with the new garbage disposal procedure being

initiated in the Kasbah, the alley cats are dying like flies. I won't miss the noise they make, fighting and fornicating over the roofs of the Arab quarter through the night. In their absence the rats will strut.

April 1

Dinner with the Bowleses in Jane's apartment. The spontaneous affection and sense of fun they share make them seem more like brother and sister than man and wife. Their intimacy is more fraternal than sexual. They live in separate apartments, one above the other, and communicate by a squeaking mauve toy telephone. Jane: "Fluffy, (squeak) come on up. John and Joe are here. Dinner (squeak) is ready." Jane likes to cook. Tonight it was jugged hare in a red wine sauce. It was like being in New York except for Sherifa[1] who rattled on in Arabic in her gruff mannish voice and laughed uproariously at her own jokes. A rough alien presence who acted as though she owned the place. Jane—a fragile figure like a priceless vase that has been knocked to the floor. The pieces have been glued back together, but crudely and the cracks show. Sherifa stood there, arms crossed, hammer in hand.

April 2

I have written a novel . . . far too soon. I should have waited, but I couldn't stop. Now I'm anxious to begin another.

April 7 - Marrakesh, Hôtel Central Annexe, Restaurant Rex

Tea with Maurice Doan in the Djemaa el Fna. This elegant oriental had no sooner dismounted from his bike and taken his seat at the table than a shoeshine boy had his box under his expensive Italian loafer—more like a foot-glove than a shoe. The waiter had already brought

---

1. Jane Bowles' Moroccan companion.

his scented brew before we had a chance to order ours. According to our neighbour in the Kasbah, Jim Wyllie—source of all humour and gossip—Maurice and his brother Raymond have laid a trap to ensnare Barbara Hutton and her millions. The scheme, hatched in a coffeeshop and overheard by Margaret Nairn, wife of the British Consul General in Tangier, who happened to be sitting in the next booth, has already been set in motion. The Doan brothers claim their father is a Laotian Prince, while everybody knows their French mother runs a dry-cleaning establishment in Marrakesh. They aim to get rich quick off the poor little rich girl in the Kasbah.

Maurice pedaled away through the teeming mob back to his antique shop. I liked him—an effete, soft-spoken, slender oriental. He and his brother may be con men, but they come across as cultivated spiritualists.

April 16 - Erfoud, Hôtel Azizi

A stomach bug has laid me low. This is my first encounter with Saharan Africa since the trip through Tunisia and Libya two years ago. Great mountains of yellow sand (Erg Chebbi) shimmer in the distance. Eerie. I plan to cross the desert again, but not today.

April 17

Erfoud where, on an evening stroll, one passes from one part of the road heavily scented by wisteria to another stinking of a dead dog in the gutter.

July 7 - Tangier

Went to the *moussem* at Sidi Kacem with Jane Bowles and her Moroccan entourage. Joe, Jane, and I wandered through the olive grove, taking in the dervish music and fevered dancing. The Moroccans were going into trances, weaving and bumping to the drums, rolling in the dust, moaning and crying, with only the whites of their eyes showing. All under a full moon, with an eclipse casting an eerie spell. The flat plain was drenched in moonlight, with horses and donkeys standing mute and motionless as statues. The miracle of dawn coming on. I walked to the beach to watch the Moroccans gallop their horses into the sea. A light breeze, the sand cool, the sun a big red pomegranate balanced on top of a hill. Then back to the olive trees for more flute music and dancing. We found Jane asleep in a tent with Sherifa and about a dozen other Moroccan women rolled up like so many bundles of laundry. Jane's gimpy leg stuck out from under the tent flap as stiff and as straight as Pinocchio's before the Blue Fairy changed him into a real boy.

Out on the plain one of the beats was going crazy—throwing rocks.

July 16

Geoffrey Wolff[1] is here on a visit. We stayed up late drinking and laughing about the times when his father, Duke Wolff, used to sleep in my bed at Princeton when I was away on hockey trips. When I got back the place stank so much I practically had to burn the sheets.

We motorcycled south to Asilah, where Paul has rented an exotic house in the old ramparts. We took Jane for a swim in the ocean, but the seaweed frightened her. In the evening we ate with our fingers, listened to music, and took in the stars—kiffed-up stars that revolved, changed colours, and winked on and off. About 4AM Wolff and I went for a walk along the sea wall. Dogs were snarling and howling all over the village. We scurried home and gratefully watched the sun rise while the waves pounded

1. John Hopkins' roommate at Princeton University; author of *Bad Debts*; *Black Sun*, *The Brief Transit and Violent Eclipse of Harry Crosby*; *The Duke of Deception*; *Providence*; *The Final Club*; *A Day at the Beach*, and other books.

against the ramparts. By day gangs of kids rule the streets of Asilah. It's like a scene from *Suddenly Last Summer*.

July 25

Tonight I saw the most enormous shooting star disintegrate over the Strait. The trail it left in the sky lasted longer than the star itself. It is easy to write now.

August 3 - Merida, Spain

As our house in Tangier has been rented, Joe and I are motorcycling through Spain. The weather here dry and cool, reminding me of Cuzco. We asthmatics are sensitive to the quality of air, and in this climate, like the desert's, I breathe easily.

August 5 - Salamanca

We have come here to visit the university where Miguel de Unamuno confronted the fascists. I am reading his *The Tragic Sense of Life*: "God is not the cause, but the consequence of man's longing for immortality."

Today I bought a leather briefcase—a present for my 25th birthday. Spanish women in black watch silently from doorways and windows as I bargain with the leatherman.

August 6

On steeples and high places perch the nests of storks. The young ones—orange beaked—slap their wings in preparation for the flight back to Morocco. I will soon follow, *in'shallah*!

Spanish women love their children, wear black, never smoke.

August 22 - back in Tanja

Art show at the Casino de Tanger. An exhibition of paintings by Raymond Doan. Half-Laotian, half-French, he looks like the Orient's answer to Jack Palance. According to Jim Wyllie, the art show is part of the scheme orchestrated by Raymond and his brother Maurice to lure Barbara Hutton from her palace in the Kasbah. She was conned into buying *all* of Raymond's paintings.

August 25

As our house in the Kasbah is still rented, we have moved into Molly Kemsley's temporarily vacant flat in Sidi Bujari. The closets are crammed with exotic clothes: gold shoes, lizard shoes, embroidered kaftans and robes of every description. Never saw such gaudy outfits.

Yesterday there was a loud knock. Raymond Doan come to collect his duds! One doesn't generally associate orientals with emotion, but Raymond was positively panting with excitement. "I'm going to the Kasbah!" he kept repeating as he gathered up the clothes by the armful. "I'm going to the Kasbah!"

Outside, the big green Roller was purring.

Today we saw him racing a brand new E-type Jag through the narrow alleys of the Kasbah. Old graybeards had to flatten up against walls, street urchins dived down holes as the money-crazed oriental roared past.

So, the trap was laid, the bait was taken, and now he's where he wants to be—in her house, frolicking in her bed and in her bankroll.

October 15 - The American Hospital in Paris

Professeur Merle d'Aubigné has just opened my knee to discover osteochrondritis dessicans, result of an old ice hockey injury at Princeton. Reading *Catch 22* by Joseph Heller: laughter is the best cure.

October 29 - Tangier

Motorcycle accident this morning. Nearly got myself

killed. White Nile a wreck. Broadsided by a teacher from the driving school. Feeling guilty, he bought me a lottery ticket while we waited outside the police station. Can't recognize my handwriting. Still shaking. So clear today. Sea clipping sky evenly. Would like to walk on that line. When I read Camus I feel embarrassed by my lack of courage.

November 3

Torrents of rain, sealing me off in the house. I look out, furtively. I need a warmer and drier place to spend these Moroccan winters—somewhere I can breathe. The desert. I am working on a short story about asthma and loneliness in Tangier that I am calling *All I Wanted Was Company*.

November 7 - 50th anniversary of Camus' birth

A perfect day for Tangier: sunny and cloudless. The squat little ferry from Gib with its orange smokestack looks like a toy boat in the bathtub.

Blood red towel hanging against blue Moroccan sky.

The next novel: make it hard and bare, like rock in the desert.

November 10

Yesterday a photograph by Robert Freson in the Kasbah for *Esquire* with Bill Burroughs, Paul and Jane Bowles, Joe McPhillips, Omar Pound,[1] Christopher Wanklyn[2] and Emilio Sanz, a Spanish writer. This is so-called "literary Tangier."

Burroughs, monkish in his black suit and skull cap, moaned: "If this were the 1930s, I'd be in Shanghai."

Paul: "Tangier is out of the mainstream. It's a backwater. It has changed less than most places, or is changing more slowly."

1. Son of Ezra Pound, and headmaster at the American School.
2. Canadian writer and artist living in Tangier.

Grumbled Burroughs: "Tangier wins by default."

November 23

This evening about eight o'clock I went out to buy a pack of cigarettes. Passing through the Kasbah gate I realized that the medina, normally so boisterous at that hour, had grown eerily still. It was weird. The streets were empty, the children subdued. Then I heard the news: President Kennedy assassinated! The horror. A chill came over me. I ran back home and got on the phone.

Nov 27 - Marbella

Joe and I are staying with Jamie Caffery[1] in his little house at 6 Calle Haza Mesón. An expert horticulturist, Jamie's hobbies include needle-pointing, Proust (he has read *Remembrance of Things Past* over and over) and drinking. Mainly the latter. Every night we spend in the gypsy dives, listening to flamenco.

November 28

The precision of the Spanish guitar above the well of emotion that is the song. The key to freedom is solitude.

December 16

Like Proust, I envy those who live by instinct.

December 21

The phone rings ten times a day. It's Jane, in a complete tizz over her party, like a debutante before the big night.

"Jesus, how do you make a dip?"

"Sausages or meatballs?"

"Do you think I ought to invite Bill Burroughs? You

---

1. An American from Louisiana who came to Morocco with David Herbert (see footnote p. 104) and spent twelve years in Tangier before moving to Spain.

know the way he drinks!"

"Oh, God, I haven't given a party since 1955!"

December 23

Couscous at Sherifa's. Some people say Sherifa is poisoning Jane to get more money out of her, but I think Jane loves Sherifa, or a part of Sherifa no one else knows about, a part which she hopes exists but may not. Maybe it's a love potion that Sherifa's been feeding her. Sherifa's couscous was delicious.

December 27

My novel *Christopher* refused by John Murray in London. On to the next project.

December 28

Jane's do had the subdued atmosphere of a New York dinner party. Half the people were strangers nobody had ever seen before. But the food! Everything Jane serves is perfection. Oysters from Oualidia, *poussin de bois* (code name for partridge sold under the counter at the market), French champagne. Burroughs turned up in his undertaker's outfit: black suit, white shirt, narrow black tie, black shoes. Jane was relieved. He behaved like a gentleman.

What most people don't realise is that Bill is a gent, a rather old-fashioned one at that. He comes from an old, well-to-do, and well-known St. Louis family. Harvard-educated. It's part of the message he wants, subliminally, to convey. The gentleman junkie.

December 30

My mother and stepfather are staying at the Minzah. Joe and I blocked off the street by our house and hired two Moroccan bands for a party in the Kasbah. Moroccan children came by the dozen and danced like dervishes. In the midst of these festivities old Mr. Pinto approached my mother.

"Mrs. Wattles," he asked, "have you and your husband bought *round trip tickets* to Tangier?"

"I think so," my mother squeaked, alarmed by the Jewish gentleman's cadaverous appearance and deep hollow voice. "Why do you ask?"

"Because many people come to Tangier for the day or the weekend, and they like it so much *they never leave.*"

December 31/January 1

New Year's Eve dinner at the Minzah, courtesy of my stepfather.

RÉVEILLON DE LA SAINT-SYLVESTRE

Le Caviar d'Iran
Les Toasts Dorés

Le Tortue Clair en Tasse
Les Délices de Sole Alexandra

La Poularde de Bresse Soufflée «El Minzah»
La Bouquetière de Légumes

Le Médaillon de Foie Gras du Périgord

La Salade Vendôme

La Coupe de Glace aux Pralines

Les Frivolités du Père Janvier

Les Beaux Fruits du Souss

Le Double Moka

Moët et Chandon Brut Impérial

TANGER LE 31 DÉCEMBRE 1963

Prix: DH120 (about $24)
Champagne, Cotillons, Attractions
Service et Taxe compris

And that includes belly dancers, fire eaters, sword swal-
lowers, acrobats, snake charmers *et al! Bonne année!*

1964

January 5

Tangier is a lax place. Too much dope and too many servants. Food is fresh, booze is cheap, and rents are low. The weather's warm and the beach is near. *¡En otras palabras, paraiso!*

January 6

I see a man alone, astride the horizon. Go on, take the next step—get lost in the desert!

January 7

Today a sky so blue. A few white buildings and a lone tree seem to speak of impending solitude as I prepare to leave for the Sahara.

January 8

People go into the desert for a number of reasons. To be terrified, to be purified, to experience what the French call the "baptism of solitude." I go to be alone and lonely: to force myself to experience that. Also to see my muscles contract under skin and over bones. And to throw off the routine of living comfortably among friends and doing the same thing every day.

January 9

One must write, not off the cream of one's imagination, but from the very dregs of one's soul.

By that measure my writing is totally frivolous.

Carla's apartment on Boulevard de Paris consists of a bedroom, a kitchen, a bath, and a living room. The walls are hung with the paintings of artists she knew in Paris. There are a day bed and two easy chairs austerely upholstered in white Moroccan wool. Carla sits cross-legged on the floor, Moroccan-style, never in a chair. A low bookshelf holds white, hand-cut French paperbacks.

Sprinkled about the room are the souvenirs of her travels, each with its spiritual connotation: the cranium from a lamasery in Ladakh; a string of Buddhist prayer beads—each bead a tiny skull carved from human bone.

There is about Carla an aura of sadness that comes, perhaps, from having lived so many years alone. Her yearning for the unattainable overflows onto the physical side, manifesting itself in a sensual explicitness and almost manic obsession with how things taste, feel and smell.

Carla smokes Boyards and Gitanes. She drinks Moroccan wine, Scotch, Guinness, and Fundador. The black market operates freely in Tangier. Bootleggers smuggle in cigarettes and whiskey from Gibraltar. White Horse scotch costs two dollars a bottle, Fundador a dollar. A bottle of wine is less than a dollar.

Just as her childish handwriting belies her sophistication, Carla speaks French with an American accent which gives the impression she has just learned the language when in fact she's fluent. In Paris she translated Sybille Bedford's *The Legacy* into French; in New York she worked sporadically on a translation of Benjamin Constant's journals.

January 12 - First night out - Casablanca, Hôtel George V, Avenue de la Grande Armée. 10 dirhams.[1] Not bad—clean.

The feeling of melancholy induced by travelling by train

---

1. About $2.00.

at night revives childhood memories of lying alone in a hospital ward, also at night. You are alone among strangers, confined to a space you cannot leave. Your fate is in the hands of others. There is a helplessness or passivity in both situations.

January 14 Tiznit - Hôtel Belle Vue. 8 DH.
~~Good excellent~~ *wonderful! (A flush toilet).*

Yesterday a fifteen hr. bus trip from Casablanca—fifteen hours of continuous theatre. At least 200 Moroccans with their children and animals must have gotten on and off. And the land becoming drier and the horizon more distant as we head south.

January 14 1/2 - Sleepless in Tiznit

Here is unbroken flatness beyond the ramparts. The wind is blowing: the dust is swirling and entering everywhere. The Anti Atlas Mountains shimmer in the distance.

Before you can say you have lived, you have to sit around African bus terminals at five o'clock in the morning.

January 15 - Tafraoute, Hôtel Salama. 6 DH. Filthy.

Living on oranges, black bread and tea.

Paul has given me a letter to a tribal princess who owns a fortress in these mountains, but I can't find her. Only one bus per week goes anywhere near her Kasbah, and it left yesterday.

In crowded Paris I found being alone an agony. In Africa, where nature dominates, I am all right. Yesterday, wandering in the mountains around Tafraoute, I spied a flock of goats in a valley below. The wind bore the sound of a flute. Out there among the red rocks . . . complete silence. Now I know why the Greeks idealized him. (I never really understood until I heard his music.) He was about 10 years old, in a djellaba. Ramadan begins tomorrow.

January 16

Nazlie Nour, half-French, half-Egyptian hippy living in Tafraoute with her 7-yr. old son, Juba. Terrified underneath, she avoids the world. Paints, writes, says she has directed movies. Running scared from the Bomb, society, just about everything.

Leaving her house, I stepped into the ink bottle. No moon or star, not a single light shining in the village. I groped my way back to dirty sheets as invisible pariahs snapped at my heels.

January 18 - Goulimine, Hôtel des Voyageurs. 5 DH. No water.

Flat here, empty, nothing. *Waloo*. I sit in my fleabag hotel room reading about Rimbaud's grandfather, waiting for tomorrow's market! Why? The smell of human shit on the wind. Ramadan—can't get any tea. Turning into an orange, I've eaten so many.

January 19 - Goulimine - the garbage dump of the Sahara.

Spent my last night in Tiznit at the *hammam*—one of man's great inventions. Scrubbed, stretched, flipped about like a fish by an enormous Negro. Never been so clean in my life. Saw myself in the mirror: the ribs have come back.

This afternoon I climbed a gray mountain covered with sharp reddish rocks. Place full of vipers—short fat snakes with flat heads. So lazy they didn't hiss or try to get out of the way. If you step on one it turns its head and sinks its fangs into your ankle. Be careful or you're a dead man.

January 20 - Tarhjijt, Hôtel ? (no name) 2 DH for a straw mat.

This oasis comes close to paradise. In the middle of a landscape of shiny black rock—palm trees full of dates, grass, little canals, paths, sunken dikes. Little black birds with orange beaks flit through air that is both warm and cool. Few people are about and few dwellings are to be seen—palms and mud walls hide all. Occasionally I glimpse a woman in black, shouldering a jug of water, gliding through the palms. I hear children laughing among the trees. Water runs in little canals—*seguiat*. Having found the serpent, I'm looking for Eve. The serpent is an American mining engineer called Mr. Anderson who is about to let loose a monster—one that will strangle and crush this place. He says there is pure magnesium here. The whole area is a huge crater where a gigantic comet hit the earth millions of years ago. By some freak of nature the magnesium has refined itself—eight million tons of it and worth $32,000 a ton! Next year an American mining company, Johns Manville, is moving in. This is the way the world will end—exploited and industrialized.

January 21

Camping on jungle riverbanks in Peru left me with a fear of snakes. Last night I slept with a candle burning, lest one slither in and take me by surprise. The oasis swarms with adders, cobras, scorpions, but . . . the best dates in the world.

January 22

I keep Ramadan as a matter of courtesy, and to avoid dirty looks should I light up a cigarette to kill my hunger. "*Tu ne fais pas Ramadan, Monsieur?*" They are so strict in their habits that even a Christian must be a good Moslem while travelling in the south of Morocco during the month of Ramadan.

January 22 1/2, 2:07 AM (still can't sleep)

To do what Rimbaud did with his poetry, to go beyond doubt, reflections and questioning—to a level of pure sensation, to make poetry ecstasy. He gave up and went to Harar; I'm in this place.

January 23

The Berbers never use *vous* when they speak French, using only the familiar *tu*. From their life outdoors they have got something great which I hope they never lose, despite Anderson and his factories. He too appreciates their qualities. Hardest and most grateful workers he has ever seen. They hate Arabs (Northerners). His men hid a live cobra under the clothes of a union man from Casa while he was swimming. He got the message and cleared out.

January 23 1/2

Back in Tiznit, weak from lack of food.

Saw a face this afternoon identical to the one looking out from Velazquez's *Bacchus*. The direct simplicity of these people.

January 24 - Aqqa

Arrived here feeling sick, thin, wiry, strong. The Sahara: cold, windy, dusty, lonely, lovely. The call to prayer echoes from a distant mosque. Dust everywhere. The dust is six inches deep. Your feet kick up explosions when you walk. On the bus we cover our faces with black *fibrans* to keep from choking.

Berber men squat while pissing, bearing out Montaigne.

January 25 - Aqqa

This place is a ghost town. There's nobody here. The old Foreign Legion fort seems deserted. Last night I shared a *tajine* with the bus drivers. The Berbers are simple, honest and fatalistic; they make us Westerners seem neurotic, grasping at straws. They know that fate lies not down the road ahead, but behind us, written by the hand of God—*Mektoub*. They seem wiser and happier. They take life as it comes and—*in'shallah*—make the best of it. If I am to learn something on this trip it will be from them.

January 26

Everyone black here: high cheekbones, broad cheeks, narrow nose bridges, nostrils flaring out like funnels. These are the Haratine people, descendants of slaves dragged in chains across the burning wastes of the Sahara to work in the oases of the Moroccan south.

January 27

Against the wall of the old Foreign Legion fort stands a row of native barber shops. Each is identically equipped with a decrepit deck chair, charcoal brazier (fanned by an infant helper) for heating water, and a once colourful beach umbrella to shade the client from the African sun. Offering their services to the Moroccan army, the barbers trim the soldiers' beards and moustaches. Saharan men, I have observed, routinely shave their heads. This wards off ringworm and keeps the scalp clean and comfortable during long airless periods beneath the turban.

Taking a seat in one of the tottering chairs, I unwrapped yards of cloth from my head. Stropping his blade on a leather strap, the barber sized me up as a small crowd of women and children gathered to watch the *nazrani* having his head shaved. The straight razor scraped on my scalp, and my hair fell to earth. A woman snatched it up. The barber, with a mischievous grin, held up a cracked mirror for me to see. One side of my head was an ugly grayish egg while on the other hair still grew.

A tear slid down my cheek! Wiping it away, I ordered him to finish the job. Afterwards I listened to a lecture on how to massage the naked scalp with hot olive oil so the hair will grow back thick and strong.

January 31 - Taroudannt Hôtel. 6 DH.
Comfortable, if you can bear the colours.

This is Souss country—rich—with markets and shops

bursting with produce. It is also full of *colons*—tough, self-confident French running their farms, leading a man's life, reminding me of white settlers in Kenya. I'm staying in a French hotel and, faced with lunch, I ate it—the first European meal in three weeks.

Already I miss the Sahara. What is it about that blasted lunar landscape, where I felt so sick and lonely, that makes me want to run back into it? How I long for a sea of yellow sand!

As I head north toward Tangier, I already feel a deep nostalgia over having left something pure behind. That purity was me.

February 2 - Taroudannt

Having missed the bus from Ait Melloul, I was picked up by a man in a hurry—a Franciscan monk who took pity on me as I stood forlornly on the roadside with my wicker suitcase. As we raced through the orange groves in his little VW, I asked him to explain the difference between our god and theirs.

His reply: "There is no difference; the difference is us."

February 3

The Berber is a kind of ideal among men. He seems to be perpetually alone, even in the company of other men. Neither does he attempt to evade his elemental solitude, which he accepts as fate. He is generous, polite, curious, modest and hospitable. Nothing is assumed except that you will be the same.

February 4

I don't look forward to going back to Tangier and taking up my old habits again. Tonight—my last south of the Atlas—I shared a *tajine* and sipped tea with a crowd of Moroccans in a dirty restaurant. I felt sublimely free and can see the point in going native.

Everyone in this town is living alone.

February 7
Paul Bowles has produced a tremendous body of work. Last night he admitted he is not interested in flesh and blood characters, but in people as fictional expressions of ideas, etc. Situations and ideas interest him more than people, as they did Camus.

February 8
Finished *The Naked Lunch*, the wildest, funniest book I've ever read.

February 9
Every Friday a black flag flies from the mosque outside my window. It inspires a kind of dread in me, like a pirate ship's Jolly Roger. It also reminds me how quickly the weeks are passing.

February 11
Memories of Libya: God-dammit! You get on that motorcycle as the sun comes up and head out across the desert with your arms and legs free. You go as far as you want and as fast as you want. The point is never to stop.

February 15 - Ketama (Kif capital of the world)
La Estrella del Norte (our bus) got stuck in the snow and the motor conked out. Joe and I had to spend the night in a road mender's cabin. My feet were soaked until we got the fire going. Slept like a couple of dogs in front of the fire while the blizzard howled outside.

March 27 (Joe's birthday) - in Sevilla for Semana Santa

Jamie Caffery picked us up on the Algeciras dock, and we drove here in his little car, stopping at every bar along the way. Jamie, a Catholic, belongs to El Gran Poder, one of the marching orders that carries the statue of the Virgin (La Macarena) through the streets. Following the procession, we dive into one bar after another, all of them seedy low-life joints where Jamie feels free and anonymous.

March 31

Tangier addles the complacent lives of middle-class Americans. The city's tolerance of people, their religions and vices, its international quality, and the babble of languages tends morally and culturally to unhinge Americans with a tendency to pigeonhole and categorize.

April 5 - Ain Sefra, Algeria

On Paul's recommendation we have come to this place where Isabelle Eberhardt drowned in a flash flood sixty years ago.

April 11 - Tangier

Today the Kasbah was invaded by a boatload of blazered, capped, stripe-tied, knee-socked English school children on vacation. Never saw such crazy kids. Redheaded, towheaded, thick glasses, peering, gaping agog at everything from mules to Arabs. In America they would be branded as weenies, but I see no reason to worry over England's future generations. They have preserved their character, their eccentricities, their curiosity.

Outside my window sitting atop a high wall, an Arab girl, her robe in tatters, her face ravaged by syphilis, watches these healthy, affluent children and in turn is watched by me.

Returned to the Kasbah to find a letter from Sonia Orwell at *Art and Literature* magazine in Lausanne. She has accepted my short story *All I Wanted Was Company* and enclosed a check for $400! All thanks to Paul. He read the story and suggested I send it in.

I went to tell Paul the news and found Burroughs. He didn't say much, just sat in the corner dipping his hand into the *majoun* jar, like a kid eating jam with his fingers. Later Carla, Joe and I ran into him again dining alone in the cellar at Paname's. This time he regaled us with tales of his Peruvian adventures. His dry laconic delivery had us shrieking with laughter.

Many nights he sits at the Parade Bar having dinner before the regulars arrive. He likes good food. A lonely ascetic figure in a dark business suit, he generally eats by himself staring poker-faced at the wall. When I bring my drink to his table, he always asks me to sit down. The undertaker look puts people off, but like all writers he works alone all day and enjoys socializing in the evening.

April 23

Carla has introduced me to the works of Celine. She loves him not only for his black sense of humour but also because, as a "slum doctor", he practised medicine in the poorest parts of Paris. Carla's sympathies go out, like an arrow, to the desperate and the down-trodden, the poor and the pathetic.

May 6

Among Tangier's ageing expatriate population, death is common (they say they bury them two deep at St. Andrew's English Church), but no one is ever born here, and marriage is rare. People spend the second halves of their lives in Tangier. If the pattern continues, the foreign community must eventually wither and die.

June 14

Richard Hughes, Robin Maugham, Margaret Lane—all these English writers gravitate to Zero, Place de la Kasbah, where they sit beneath Samuel Pepys' fig tree while Jim Wyllie spins yarns of the Morocco that was.

Yesterday he told Margaret and me about the time when he was briefly a slave owner. It happened back in 1914 or thereabouts when Jim had been sent to Safi to learn Arabic and explored southern Morocco on horseback. He was staying with a friendly Caid in the Atlas and, when it came time to leave, his host presented him with a slave to lead him out of the mountains. As it would have been impolite to refuse, Jim said he would send the boy back when he reached safety.

"No, no. He's yours to keep," the Caid insisted. "Mamadu wants to see the world. Who better to show it to him than you? Farewell, Jim."

And so forth. Off they went, and it was hard going. When they got to the Oued Dadès, Jim said, "You're a free man, Mamadu, we're in French territory now."

The slave was indignant. "Sidi Jim," he said, "who caught you when you fell off your horse? Who baked your bread in the sand dunes of Morocco? Your bones would be there now, crunched by the jackals, if it weren't for me. You're my master—you can't abandon me like this!"

Jim told him he wasn't abandoning him. In gratitude for everything he had done for him, he was giving him his freedom.

The slave was crestfallen. "Is this the reward I get for saving your life?"

"What greater gift is there than freedom?" Jim asked.

But Mamadu thought Jim was mocking him.

57

"Sidi Jim," he said, "all my life I have been protected, housed, clothed, and treated as a respected member of Sidi Mohammed's household. Now you throw me out!"

"Don't you want to be free?" Jim asked.

"What is this freedom?" the slave replied. "I want food and new clothes. White bread and a roof over my head. A master to pick a bride and pay for my marriage. I swear on my mother's unmarked grave, I would rather die of thirst in the Grand Sahara than be free!"

Jim had a heck of a time getting rid of the guy. He finally handed him over to the commander of the French Foreign Legion garrison at Skoura, who took him on as a house servant.

Richard Hughes wants Jim to write down his adventures and publish them, but so far Jim has only produced a slim volume of Moroccan stories for children. Because of Jim, Margaret Lane has fallen in love with Morocco and is buying a house here.

June 20

Tangier street vendor, master of the hard sell, persuading:
    the shoeless to buy his socks,
       " illiterate "   "   " ball pt. pens,
      " penniless "   "   " wallets.

July 6

I gradually work myself, through a period of protracted concentration, into a state of receptivity where the seminal idea for the next book becomes inevitable. These days of apparent inactivity, with my mind in neutral, often turn out to be the most productive.

As Burroughs says, "Your mind will answer most questions if you learn to relax and wait for the answer. Like one of those thinking machines, you feed in the question, sit back, and wait. . . ."

[Hopkins and McPhillips spent the next month travelling in South America.]

August 15

Back from our summer jaunt to Peru, Joe and I walked into the Parade to find Burroughs sitting at the bar.

"Howdy, boys," he offered in his dry nasal drawl. "I thought you two were floating down the Amazon on a balsa raft. Haw, haw, haw."

Sitting beside him was a tall pale man who studied us with a blue, hypnotic gaze.

This turned out to be Brion Gysin,[1] legendary painter, poet, inventor of the Dream Machine, Burroughs' friend and collaborator who introduced him to the so-called "cut-up technique."

August 23

Irving Rosenthal[2] entered Paul's apartment, screamed, and covered his eyes with his hands.

"What's wrong?" Paul asked.

"That thing in the cage! What is it?"

"A parrot."

"I've never seen one before! Take it away!"

Ira Cohen:[3] "I know he is guilty, but I am not sure of what."

---

1. Author of *The Third Mind*, (with William Burroughs); *The Process*; *The Last Museum*, and *Here To Go*.
2. Editor of *Big Table*, the literary magazine, where excerpts of *The Naked Lunch* first appeared, and author of *Sheeper*.
3. American poet and photographer. He edited and published the single issue of *Gnaoua*, a magazine of Tangier writers.

Norman Glass:[1] filing a lawsuit against his mother "for being a Jew."

Tangier is a magnet for wandering artists and writers. They all migrate to Paul's apartment.

August 24 - Villa Gazebo, 282 Monte Viejo

We have moved from the Kasbah to the Old Mountain. A red-tiled, blue-shuttered, whitewashed house belonging to Marguerite McBey.[2] I think Alan Sillitoe wrote *The Loneliness of the Long Distance Runner* here. A wide terrace and large garden (more of a wood than a garden), with a 180° view of the Strait and the coast of Spain. A tower to write in. *¡Paraiso!*

August 25

A bang on the door. It's Burroughs, pink copy of *The Financial Times* under his arm, with Anthony Balch, a cameraman. They were making a film and wanted a shot of Bill talking to Coco, the parrot. Afterwards we walked in the wood.

Burroughs: "Nice place you've got here."

"Reminds me of the South American rain forest."

"Must be a smugglers' nest."

"I bet there are squirrels and rabbits in these woods—wish I had my gun."

"Your neighbours' dog out there, it wanted to eat me. You ought to have that dog put away. Mix iron filings with his food—that's how the Moroccans do it."

August 27

Paul has rented the Bonnet cliff house for the summer.

---

1. English writer and translator of Gerard de Nerval's *Journey to the Orient*.
2. Widow of the Scottish etcher and painter, James McBey. (See pages 212-213)

Jane brings food baskets from town. Tennessee Williams was there, so overcome with sadness over the death of his friend Frank Merlo that he hardly spoke.

Last night Paul, Brion Gysin, Joe McPhillips and I watched Larbi Layachi[1] make *majoun*. Larbi's recipe calls for chopped almonds and walnuts, honey from his father's beehives, and a small mountain of kif. Later we walked to the cliff. White waves sucked at the rocks below. A big moon hanging over the Strait left a slippery track on the water.

Brion: "We're here to go."
Paul: "We're here to learn."

August 28

Everyone was in the Parade last night—Tennessee Williams, Brion Gysin, Burroughs.

"Bill, I thought you were leaving."
"Man, there is no place to go! Jay, mix this boy another bourbon mist, with a twist."

September 6

A novel as hard as bare and as distinct as a rock in the desert.

November 4

Pirate flags swing in a whitewashed sky. VIVA TANGER signs are up all over town. (I never found out why.)

November 6

Tangier winter: on the beach before the drenched gray silent city two ragged Arabs shovel wet sand into straw sacks astraddle sick white mules. Clank of shovels.

---

1. Author of *A Life Full of Holes*—written under the pen name Driss ben Hamed Charhadi and translated from Arabic by Paul Bowles.

When I go to Paul's I knock on his door about midnight and stay until two or three. We go up on the roof to look at the stars, listen to music, talk. Paul is an attentive host during these late night sessions and deftly anticipates the effects of the weed he loves to smoke. When you get the munchies, he produces a box of cookies or a bowl of fruit. When the pipe makes you so thirsty your throat begins to feel like the inside of a tin cup, he serves Lapsang Souchong with lemon and sugar. When there's a gap, something missing—you're too spaced out to know what it is—he lights a joss stick dipped in some magic ointment brought back from the Orient. (He has a cupboard full of exotic scents.) When the room lapses into silence you are aroused by the sound of bells, tiny bells that tinkle delicately in a Thai temple which he has just put on the machine.

Paul loves games, especially word games. Last night we dreamed up a series of new languages:

Franish and Spench.

Hebic and Arabrew. (This one was Paul's.)

Dussian and Rutch.

Grulgarian and Beek.

Feedish and Swinnish.

Afterwards I walk home through Sidi Bujari and Dradeb. My solitary footsteps echo through the deserted alleys of another world. On the top of a wall a cat picks its way among speckled points of broken glass. Up the Old Mountain road beneath the eucalyptus trees. Muffled whispers from the sea. Feeble street lamps let down a flickering light. The mystery lies behind the high stone walls.

Paul's idea, having heard me talk about my raft trip down the Amazon, is to use the jungle river as a setting for my new novel. A continual progression: the flow of the river, change in scenery, time, thought and action.

"Boy, never underestimate the opposition." W. Burroughs on his encounter with Protestant missionaries in Peru. "Among them a man has to take a drink on the sly. They don't like to see a man take a drink."

December 23 - with Joe and Carla in Kairouan, Tunisia

Cold N. African winter. Weary travellers try to keep warm in an unheated Arab hotel. Dogs talking in the still chill night. Right out of Gide, but the truth.

December 26 - Island of Djerba, Tunisia

Turkish fort, pink in the morning sun, human shit clotting the battlements, turning back into the soil. Arab boys crawl from holes in the walls, hang around like jackals, waiting for a sign. An old fisherman casts his net in dead calm early morning water.

The island: palm trees raise their heads like sea serpents from the shimmering quicksilver mirage. Beaches caked with mounds of gray seaweed. Smell of rotten sponges. A one-legged fisherman, sprawled in a courtyard in the afternoon sun, keeps an eye on his sponges drying on the line. Stamping of mules.

1965

January 1 - Island of Djerba, Tunisia

We spent New Year's Eve in the coffee houses of Houmt-Souk, drinking coffee laced with fig wine and playing slapjack with Arabs and Jews.

February 2 - Tangier

Teaching all day and staying up half the night making notes for the next novel.

February 26

Like most expatriates in Tangier my Spanish teacher has a colourful past. Prior to the Civil War Doña Elena Spencer studied medicine in Madrid, where she revelled in the heady intellectual and cultural atmosphere that marked the last days of the Republic. When war broke out, she was so horrified by the atrocities committed on both sides that she fled to Tangier. Disillusioned by man's inhumanity to man, she vowed never to practice medicine and supported herself teaching Spanish at the American Consulate. Independent, intellectual, also a brilliant cook. Every Friday evening after school Joe and I meet at her flat on Calle Victor Hugo to talk Spanish and eat: *ajo blanco*—a cold almond and garlic soup sprinkled with peeled green grapes; *criadillas*—sliced sheep's testicles fried in bread crumbs; *croquetas de pollo,* similarly fried, to name a few of her Andalucian specialities, which we wash down with Diamante and Paternina wines, but mainly with many *ginebra y tonicas*.

Despite our boozy supper, she doesn't let us forget our lesson, and the talk turned to animals. I asked her what the Spanish word for quadruped was. She thought about it for a minute before coming up with:

"Un pingüino."

More drinks were required, as well as more lessons in Spanish.

March 13

Listening to Jilala[1] music recorded by Brion Gysin: pain and ecstasy seem to produce the same sounds from men. The smell of art: in Gysin's case it smells of patchouli.

April 6 - Aglou Plage, near Tiznit

A boy has been lost in the sea. He went down late from the caves, after drinking a bottle of wine, to fish off the rocks in the moonlight. The tide comes in quickly here. Every year the sea claims the lives of several young men. The Moroccans say a sea witch lures them out, seducing them with her song and laughter, and gives the body back after three or four days.

At dawn the fishermen were sitting on the sand dunes, scanning the coast with binoculars. We met the boy's father, an old man with a white beard. He was ashamed that his son had been drinking wine.

After three days a cry went up. The spectacle of old men running. We came to the place where the body lay and made a circle around it. The eyes had been pecked out by gulls, the hair nibbled by fish.

The father arrived. The circle parted. He knelt by the

---

1. A Sufi cult. "To Europeans, the music of the Jilala is Moroccan folk music being played on long low-pitched transversal flutes (*shebaba*) and large flat hand drums (*bendir*); to a member of the cult, however, it is a sequence of explicit choreographic instructions, all of which are designed to bring about a state of trance, or possession." Paul Bowles, *Without Stopping*.

body and placed his djellaba over it. He did not want us to look at the body of his dead son.

A plank was brought and the body placed upon it. Chanting, the little procession moved toward the cemetery.

May 10 - Tangier

Today I have finished a short story called *The Up and the Down*. Paul likes it and is thinking about where I should send it.

May 17

Wilfred Thesiger has rented the Thomas Cooke house down the road. Having greatly admired *The Empty Quarter*, I go around for a visit, hoping to hear him expand on his Arabian adventures. But the old desert hand doesn't want to talk about the desert. He's in Tangier with his mother; the only thing that interests him is bridge and gossip.

June 22

Having quit the American School for good in order to write full-time, I have begun work on a new novel based on my adventures in Peru.

July 12

Camus, *The Rebel*: "It is not sufficient to live. There must be a destiny that does not have to wait for death."
From *The Myth of Sisyphus*: "Everything begins with lucid indifference. Then comes the evolution of caring . . . creation follows indifference and discovery."

July 13

J. F. McCrindle, editor of *Transatlantic Review*, has accepted my story *The Up and the Down*.

July 14

With Bill Burroughs in his apartment atop the Lotería Building, 16 rue Delacroix. Decrepit tables and shelves loaded with cut-ups, clippings and files. The old upright Remington looks like a dinosaur from another age. The tape recorder has only one tape: a recording of static. This comfortless place is more like a writer's factory than an author's study.

We walk onto the balcony. "This is the bridge of my battleship," he drawls. "From here I can see everything. See the Comisaría down the street? Fire one! Boom! It's gone! Haw haw haw."

His reaction to *All I Wanted Was Company*: "A non-derivative style."

August 10

Angus Wilson takes tea chez Mme. and Mlle. Gerofi, who run the Gallimard bookshop here in Sin City. *Thé à la Belge* consists of whiskey and chocolates at five o'clock in the afternoon. The library ladies are thrilled to have the distinguished *homme de lettres* in their salon.

"*Encore du whiskey, Monsieur Wilson?*" Isabelle asks in her little bird voice.

"*Avec plaisir!*" The old boy's face is getting red.

The North African sunlight pours across the terrace of their penthouse apartment. Wilson is dressed stylishly in a dove grey suit and open-necked white shirt. The shock of white hair reminds me of Robert Frost, but without the wildness. Wilson has been too long in academia.

I escort Wilson from this refined environment and flag him a taxi. Then I wobble across Parque Brooks to Bowles' concrete blockhouse behind the American Consulate. No light enters here. The terrace window is blocked by a seething mass of ugly vegetation that makes me think the Amazon forest is trying to come in and have tea with us. Mohammed M'rabet,[1] stripped to the waist, brown muscles bulging, is cutting kif with a meat axe. The music is Cuban and violent.

August 19 - A walk down the Old Mountain Road.

The bark-festooned eucalyptus trees let down a flickering light. Big square houses sit in overgrown gardens. A rustic crowd uses this road—fishermen, woodchoppers, chanting women beneath bundles of sticks, donkeys loaded with firewood, girls carrying bunches of wild flowers on their heads, shepherds and goatherds with their flocks. Occasionally one catches a glimpse of the sea.

August 25

This notion of writing full-time is a myth. No one can write full-time. I have tried writing during the day and at night. I have used alcohol to evoke the muse, which has taught me one thing: my brain operates best stone-cold sober early in the morning.

September 10

I've been too absorbed with the novel to spend much time on this journal. I work all morning, then ride the motorcycle to the Atlantic beach for a swim. After Mina's lunch I sleep for an hour, then spend the afternoon revising. Dinner usually with Gysin and/or Burroughs at the Parade followed by a midnight visit chez Bowles. How I love this creative routine!

---

1. Moroccan storyteller of Riffian parentage. His books include *Marriage with Papers*; *The Big Mirror*; *The Boy who Set the Fire*; *The Chest*; *Chocolate Creams and Dollars*; *The Lemon*; *Look and Move On*; *M'Hashish*, all transcribed and translated into English by Paul Bowles.

September 23

Ahmed Maimouni, *capataz* of the stevedores in the port, phoned to say I should come down to look at a strange ship that docked during the night. It was an old freighter whose sides had been brightly painted with flowers, birds and bumblebees. A huge Mickey Mouse adorned the smoke stack.

As a crowd of Moroccans looked on, a ramp was lowered, and out trundled a motorcade of Land Rovers and Jeeps, all decked out in the same absurd nursery colours. Then followed a sleek procession of chauffeur-driven Mercedes. From each car the back seat had been removed. In its place a padded bar had been inserted across the windows. On each bar solemnly perched a peregrine falcon, ornately hooded.

One of the princes of the House of Saud has come to play in the Moroccan desert.

November 15 - Casablanca, 11:54 PM

Having completed the first draft of my new book, *The Attempt*, a novel of Peru, I have come here on the train with Paul and Mohammed M'rabet, whose stories Paul is translating into English. We taxied from the station to the Hotel Astoria, where we left our bags. Paul was in a hurry; he didn't want to miss supper. We walked quickly to Chez Milhet on the market square. Paul is a fastidious eater. "This is the only place in Casa I feel safe," he says. (By that he means his stomach).

Tomorrow Marrakesh; then the desert.

November 21 - Tangier

Said goodbye to Paul in Marrakesh, bussed to Ouarzazate, got sick as a dog the first day (strep throat) and came straight back here.

Working every day on the second draft of *The Attempt,*
and it feels good.

1966

February 13

The Attempt absorbs all my writing energy. I have little left for this diary.

March 5

The *Queen Mary* passed through the Strait this morning. The day was so clear and calm I could read the letters on the bow through the telescope five miles away, with the white villages of Spain behind.

The novel is progressing—the first chapter has been accepted by *Art and Literature* for the preliminary publication—but the eyes are tired from writing.

Tangier—the mimosa and acanthus are in bloom. Millions of blood oranges flood the market. I look forward to uncooping myself from this room when the novel is completed.

April 10

The Greek method of drama: to seize upon an elemental human situation and bulldog it to death, until the audience is ready to cry out for mercy: *e.g.* Elektra's all-consuming hatred of her mother and her thirst for revenge; the inexorable unravelling of Oedipus's preordained fate.

"Time . . . supervisor, leading to inevitable death." *Elektra*.

May 3

The novel's finally finished. The Levante blows day and

night. I'm bored, frustrated, and want to get out.

June 7

Few works of literature have moved me as much as Joe McPhillips' production of *Oedipus the King* (W. B. Yeats translation). Aside from being an inspirational teacher and theatre director, he is a resourceful assembler of local talent: Paul Bowles wrote the music, Ira Belline[1] designed the costumes (she learned her trade working for Louis Jouvet in France), and Brion Gysin painted Greek masks on the faces of the student actors.

Unlike us, the Greeks did not feel sorry for themselves. There is a great acceptance, a great courage, a great grace. Sometimes the Moroccans come near to them in this.

July 12 - Moulay Idriss

Joe and I are staying with Joe's student, Driss Drissi, in his village on the flanks of Jebel Zerhoun. Driss is a Sherif; that is, he's a direct descendant of the Prophet Mohammed. He also traces his lineage to the Idrissis, the founding dynasty of Morocco. In America he would be equivalent of someone directly descended from Jesus Christ *and* George Washington.

The dry summer heat, the profusion of olive trees on the hillsides, the century plants pitted against the sky, the torrents of water rushing under the houses are part of a scene that has not changed for hundreds of years. Yesterday we walked to the Roman city of Volubilis. Today we trekked over the mountain to the *moussem* at Sidi Ali—14 km.

For the first time in my life asthma stopped me cold. While the others went on, I returned to the village on the back of a donkey, and drove the car to Sidi Ali. Thousands

1. Igor Stravinsky's niece. (See pages 104-107)

of tents were pitched on the hills. We sat on a wall as the Khamadcha musicians and dancers passed beneath. With us was Kraa (baldie), local muscleman recruited by Driss to defend us against any Muslim fanatic who might take offence at the presence of Christians at their religious festival. Under the willow trees by the spring we saw the followers of Aisha Kandisha—long-haired women who had covered themselves with mud. Muscle-bound Kraa turned ashen and started to make insane blubbering noises at the sight of these witchlike sirens. The dancers were throwing heavy clay pots into the air. The pots crashed on their heads. The dancers whirled around, and we were spattered with blood. I almost envied them their self-inflicted wounds and insatiable thirst for music, designed to drive out the devil and free the spirit. Bees swarmed on the *shabakia* and the mint tea.

July 13 - Fez

So many things to buy. After hours of haggling, I came away with a heavy copper tray. In the dry heat of Fez I sleep without covers at the Palais Jamai.

July 18 - Tangier

Paul gone off to Bangkok.

July 19

Tangier bores me now. I need to get out, too.

July 20

Diogenes of Oenoanda: "Nothing to fear in God, nothing to feel in Death, good can be attained, evil can be endured."

July 25

My novel *The Attempt* finally completed after many revisions.

August 5
Birthday (28th). Manuscript mailed to publishers.

September 5 - Wainscott, Long Island
The Attempt accepted by Viking Press in New York! Corlies Smith telephoned me at 10PM with the news. I had to run down to the beach and dive into black waves to cool off.

October 18 - Tanja
Cavafy's Alexandrine world has its parallel in Tangier—the café life, the relaxed Mediterranean atmosphere, the moderately productive daily routine.

December 21 - La Petite Maison, Dar Tounsi, Marrakesh
Ira Belline has rented me this mud house on her farm in the palm groves about five km. from the city ramparts. Barbara Hutton bought the property for Ira when asthma forced her to leave Tangier for this drier climate.

La Petite Maison has no telephone or electricity; I light the place with kerosene lamps whose reflecting mirrors throw a double light. A well provides cool, pure water that flows in underground channels from the Atlas. The fish swim blind down there. I have installed a pump and built a reservoir on the roof. No hot water, just an ice cold shower. Ira has painted the house white inside and Marrakesh rouge out. She has hung her paintings on the walls and laid down carpets on the cool tile floors. This rustic abode has been civilized by her loan of antique French furniture. Central heating is provided by a strong-drawing fireplace.

By day sunlight floods among the olive and orange orchards. The snow-capped peaks of the Haut Atlas are visible through the date palms. By night the pure desert silence is broken by the sound of distant drumming.

December 23

The mystery of walking through the palmeraie by night. The silence of the universe blots out the noisiness of man. Moonlight slides among the trees like sunlight of another planet. Palms rear their heads like the enormous dark flowers of another planet. One ever-present danger: the packs of rabid dogs that prowl the oasis.

December 24
Bab Al-Khemis market outside the ramparts of Marrakesh.

While I was bargaining for lanterns made out of tin cans, a Moroccan schoolboy, hoping to start a conversation, recited all the French he learned in school: *"Bonsoir, monsieur. Quelle heure est-il? La maison. La plume. Le chien. Voici le livre . . ."* etc. I let him carry my basket.

December 28

My attempts to practice my newly learned Arabic are greeted by expressions of incredulity from the Moroccans. The egg lady in the souk launched into a long monologue of which I understood not a single word. The carriage driver taking me to the Djemaa el Fna replied in perfect English, "Is that Polish you are speaking, sir, or is it Greek?"

1967

Camus:

"The loftiest work . . . maintains an equilibrium between reality and man's rejection of that reality. . . ."

"The freest art and the most rebellious will therefore be the most classical: it will reward the greatest effort."

Resistance, Rebellion, and Death.

February 6 - Tantan (Moroccan Sahara)

Extraordinarily barren tableland. Empty! Oued Draa a few stagnant pools. Where did that river in Zagora go? Swallowed by the Sahara. The people here are gentle and polite; they promenade the sand streets in blue robes that flow like water. Bluffs overlooking the town are marked by piles of stones where nomads pitch their tents when they come for the great *moussem* in June. Huge ravens float in the wind that blows all the time.

Tomorrow I go by truck to Tarfaya: 24 hrs. running or two days with stops.

Tasted camel milk today. Bitter but refreshing.

February 8 - Tarfaya

Arrived here this afternoon after a twenty hr. truck trip across the desert. So much beauty . . . so much land!

This is a Spanish ghost town at Cape Juby on the edge of nowhere (the theoretical frontier between Morocco and the Spanish Sahara). Sand dunes as high as your head impede traffic on the street (the occasional stray donkey).

Decrepit Spanish buildings with the paint peeling off, windows broken, and doors sagging and banging in the wind. Pariah dogs eat a dead porpoise on the beach. But glorious sun and beautiful sea. I swam out to le Chateau de la Mer, a fortified trading post built by the British in the nineteenth century, now deserted and gutted by the sea.

The *toba* is the Mauritanian *sebsi*, a kind of hand-engraved silver mini megaphone you fill with tobacco. It gets hot after a few drags.

February 24 - Tangier

The siren of a departing ocean liner makes me dream of Camus.

March 5

In preparation for summer the Moroccans are building grass cafés at Merkala Beach. Groups of boys lie on the sand with their heads together, making starlike patterns on the beach.

March 7

Wild children have taken over Calle Larache, where Bill Burroughs now lives. "Every year there seem to be more of them," Brion says. "Every day!" It is difficult and even dangerous to visit Bill's house. The children grow angry if their games are interrupted. Paul thinks Bill eggs them on. He pays these kids to throw stones at strangers so he can get on with his writing.

March 8

The hawks are up! Every year in early spring hundreds of hawks rise from the walls and glide in a high swirl over the Old Mountain. Always on a day of Levante. They hang motionless in the invisible gale, then peel away for Spain.

Tangier perches astride the great bird highway between Europe and Africa.

March 22 - Villa Taylor, Marrakesh

My mother has rented rooms in this fabulous mud castle. Benny Goodman and other paying guests are also staying, including Dora, the beautiful Brazilian girl. During the long hour of the siesta, while the sound of Goodman's clarinet spooks the hot silence of the colonnaded courtyard with its dripping fountain, I lie on my painted bed in my painted room fumbling with the row of tiny buttons on Dora's green kaftan. . . .

March 31

I've been put in charge of making the set for Joe McPhillips' production of Paul Bowles' play *The Garden*.

We approached a whitewashed shack surrounded by a live cane fence. Larbi pounded the top of an empty oil drum with his fist.

"That's the door bell!" he laughed.

A dog came out and barked. The cane man appeared with a son and two daughters.

"We want to buy cane."

We bargained, reached a price, and the man began to cut the cane. Pull and snap. Later, as we were stripping the cane of leaves, Mohammed M'rabet came along with a sack of oranges. He laughed and accepted one of the canes for a fishing pole. All this under a brilliant blue sky on the last day of March. We worked all day making *mamounias*, and our bare arms and faces were burnt by the African sun.

April 2

Watching Brion Gysin paint:

Brion has agreed to paint the backdrop for Paul's play *The*

Garden. Joe and I stretched a huge canvas—about 15 feet high by 30 long—and propped it up against the backboard on the basketball court at the American School. We bought the pigments he requested. Earth colours: yellow ochre, terracotta, brown, grey, etc., and green. We mixed the paints in buckets and arranged them in a row before the upright canvas. Brion had requested not paint brushes but sticks; each bucket contained the bamboo stick we mixed the paint with.

At the appointed hour the master arrived. He sat down in front of the canvas, lit his pipe and got a little stoned. He pulled from his pocket a house painter's brush, stuck it in the brown paint and like a bullfighter advanced upon the canvas. He made two sweeping arcs that looked like breasts. Then he made one long phallus-like slash of paint between them. This was supposed to be a desert scene. We wondered what he'd do next.

Then he began work in earnest. Darting along the line of buckets, he picked up the sticks and started flinging the paint onto the canvas. Quickly, he developed a technique: he directed the paint in globs or spattered the canvas with a fine rain of colour. Before our unbelieving eyes the desert came to life. Those two mounds were not breasts or balls but dunes, not sand dunes of the imagination, but the dunes of the Sahara that I have seen with my own eyes. With a flourish of green on top, that phallic stab of paint in the middle turns into a palm tree.

In a matter of minutes he covered the entire canvas with paint. There was the beleaguered palm tree in Paul's garden and the encroaching dunes. We witnessed the creation of an oasis but still couldn't comprehend how Brion did it. We marvelled at the ease, the grace, the sheer athleticism with which he brought the desert to life. The technique was carefree, but the result evoked the marching dunes that must inevitably swallow the oasis.

May 7 - In Goulimine with Dad.

The wind never stops blowing in the desert. Our footsteps quickly fill with sand. I like the sensation of being
with my father out here, of seeing how he handles the
Sahara. Divorced, separated from his children and living
alone, he visits me in Morocco once a year and has made
friends with most of my friends.

Yesterday we were invited to tea by a half-Spanish, half-
Moroccan camel driver who lives in the desert outside
Goulimine. Luis's father served with *El Tercio*[1] at Villa
Cisneros. He received us in a shack built of dead branches
and oil drums. The roof is a tent of woven goat hair. Luis
lives there with a dog, a cat and his wife. His children go to
school in the village. Camels graze about the encampment.
Shepherd boys look on from a distance: their blue robes
stand out like turquoise jewelry against the scrub, the stones
and the semi-arid mountains of the North African desert.

Tea was served by Luis' wife, a coal-black woman with
keys attached to her ears. Shrouded from head to toe, with
all but one eye covered by her voluminous blue robe, she
lays the tray before her husband and glides away mur-
muring salaams. As Luis poured out the smoking brew,
Dad sat crosslegged on the sand.

"That Luis is penniless," he told me later. "His shack
may blow away in the next sandstorm, but he has more
than I have. He has a dog, a cat, a wife and three children.
I don't have any of that."

May 10 - Tangier

The Attempt published in New York. Viking has sent me a
pile of reviews from newspapers in places like St. Paul,
Minn., Topeka, Kansas, and Omaha, Nebraska. Amazing
to think that people out there in the corn belt are reading

---

1. Spanish Foreign Legion.

my novel about Peru.

May 17

Betty Vreeland:[1] "If Joe doesn't leave Morocco this year, he'll be at the American School for the rest of his life." And I thought, well, she's probably right.

May 19

Brion in a gloomy mood: "Man, I'm bordering on the great depression! I can't remember any more how human I am, or even if I am human. The simplest problem confounds me. I seem to have forgotten everything I ever knew. I have difficulty taking the easiest, most obvious steps, in making the most straightforward statements and decisions. I don't look forward to anything . . . nothing!"

Paul on Brion: "Drugs have altered his character. He has experimented too much."

May 25

Burroughs on *The Attempt*: "I have rarely read a book that so definitely transports the reader, through the eyes of a disembodied observer, to another country."

May 29

Jews and Christians have lived side by side in North Africa for centuries, even before the Muslims arrived. There is little racism in Tangier, or evangelism from any quarter. The Spanish presence in northern Morocco was largely a lower-class one made up of refugees from Franco's civil war. Unskilled labourers mingled freely with Moroccans and learned their language as the Morcocans learned Spanish. In the south the French kept the Moroccans at arm's length, but in Tangier tolerance is taken

---

1. Wife of Frederick Vreeland, American diplomat living in Rabat.

for granted. The Tanjaouis consider themselves different from other Moroccans. For Mina, our maid, 'Morocco' begins on the outskirts of town. She regards the rest of the country as a vast, hazy plain, burning with heat and swept by violent storms, where unwashed and half-naked people wander about, babbling an incomprehensible tongue. When it comes right down to it, her view of Morocco doesn't differ much from that of most Americans.

June 17

The moon was full and the dogs were talking all over the mountain. The night was hot and the air stuffy beneath the mosquito netting. At 2AM an intruder appeared at my window, holding a knife. I awoke and lunged toward him, but he dropped away through the window. Was it a dream? The next morning I found deep footprints where the would-be thief landed in the soft garden soil.

June 20

Brion: "You have no idea what it is to die; you're too young, you can't know. You really don't believe that such a thing exists. Me, I'm beginning to see it at the end, I see myself heading toward it; I'm not so far away now."

July 5

Veronica Tennant[1] lay in the Italian Hospital, dying of emphysema. Her faithful servant Allal sat in the corner, watching and saying nothing as the loneliness of impending death swept over them. She made a noise and signalled with her fingers. Allal got to his feet and for an instant their eyes met. An hour later she was gone.

A human corpse, recently deceased, shrinks rapidly upon itself, as the flesh and bones contract upon the space

---

1. English resident in Tangier.

vacated by the departed soul. The body seems smaller with life gone out of it, and totally, utterly dead.

A pink silken handkerchief kept her jaw from dropping open. When rigor mortis had set in the nun removed it.

Yesterday Veronica's face had seemed rather puffy from cortisone; today those cheeks were sunken and pressed inwards against the jaw and teeth.

July 9

Bar Montero: Sitting at a sidewalk table a small brown Spaniard with compact peasant features, wearing a brown hat. "Gitano," they called him. Suddenly he got up and began to play the harmonica with one hand, a castanet with the other. He played one song, finished with a flourish and formally—"*Señores y señoras*"—announced the next. When he'd done he passed round the hat, then abruptly vanished. "Crazy," said a friend. "Crazy from eating too many beans!"

July 11

Brion's comments on ageing: "It's not a gradual process at all. You can go for years without changing; then in the period of a month, a week, a day, you see yourself grow old, almost visibly, before your eyes. You wake up one morning, and you really are very much older than when you went to bed. It all begins at 28 or 29, when the first wrinkles appear next to your ears."

July 22

With Timothy Leary and Louise de Meuron[1] on the Atlantic beach at midnight. Rounded hills resembled a blackened corpse sprawled beneath the moon. Tidal pools among the dunes gleamed like the obsidian eyes of some Aztec god. The wide beach bent away to the south. Tall cliffs (the

1. See p. 216.

Caves of Hercules) blocked the way north. One or two lamps twinkled from Berber villages on the hillsides. The lights of nine fishing boats dotted the sea. All of a sudden a freighter rounded the cape in a blaze of light. Leary, who had been chattering up theories all day, fell silent.

August 1

Last night on the terrace of the Gazebo, Joe and I threw a Jilala party which ended with violence. Paul and Jane came, with Jane Howard and Terence Spencer, writer and photographer for *Life*, who have been following them around Tangier. After dinner Mohammed M'rabet started dancing to the Jilala beat. He appeared to have fallen into a trance when a long curved knife materialised in his hand. He was dancing like a maniac and fell to his knees, his face a few inches from the blazing charcoal brazier. Driss and I got the knife away and tried to drag him back, but it was like wrestling ten men. In the tussle I twisted my knee, the second one that had just been operated on for an old ice hockey injury at Princeton. In the middle of the free-for-all I looked up and there was Paul. He was standing over us, cigarette holder in hand, inspecting the tangle of bodies with the detached curiosity of an entomologist watching ants grapple.

Afterwards, M'rabet and I laughed about the incident. "I feel wonderful," he said. "I feel like I am fifteen years old." In Paul's opinion I had imprudently interrupted M'rabet's Jilala dance and prevented the *Life* people from seeing an act of self-immolation; but I didn't want to see M'rabet plunge his face into that brazier of burning coals—not my friend and not in my house. Besides, M'rabet is such a ham; I think he was just showing off for the people from *Life*.

August 6

About once a week Joe and I have supper with Brion at

the Parade, Tangier's number one bar. The walls are hung with red plush curtains, and the lighting fixtures resemble old-fashioned gas lamps with gold reflecting balls. The principal decorations are three large shiny oil paintings by Stewart Church[1] depicting half-naked Nubian adolescents rowing Venetian gondolas. An awning projects over the bar, and Eugenia Bankhead's shoes (she kicked them off one night dancing on the tables) have been nailed to little platforms so no one will steal them. Lilly Kalman, the proprietress and ex-wall-of-death rider, takes pride in arranging fresh flowers every day.

Brion draws on the tablecloths, which Lilly has had framed and hung on the walls. Afterwards we end up at his place and crawl home at dawn.

August 10

Brion: glittering blue eyes, tall, thin, with pale skin that turns red when sunburnt, an extremely healthy, wiry fifty-year old. His appearance is entirely the result of his mind. Gray hair.

Despite his brilliance and insight, he is capable of some very silly things, which he admits. He's not very adept at handling his affairs, esp. financial. It may have been a mistake to have stayed so long in Tangier: the bad weather, bad luck, and especially the enormous amounts of *shira* he smokes tend to bring out the paranoia in him. And *floos*: "I've got to figure out a way to make a living. I've got to earn some money." Through a telescope on his balcony he views the ships passing down the Strait. "I ought to be on one of those ships!" he cries. "What am I doing here? But where would I go? As Bill says, Tangier wins by default. I'm spending too much money, and I don't have any to spend!"

1. Reclusive American artist living in Tangier.

August 30 - Melilla

Brion, Joe, Targuisti[1] and I have come to this place by Spanish boat from Ceuta. Brion was smoking so much hash we had to stick our heads out the portholes to breathe.

At 7PM the monsters come out, the cripples and the beggars; at eight the bouncy chicks and the boys do the *paseo*, at ten the "desperate cats" as Brion called them, take over the pavement.

Three football teams are in town, and there's no place to stay. What are we doing here? we ask ourselves. At midnight a Spanish taxi driver agreed to take us back to Tangier. We rode all night through the Rif Mountains.

We arrived at dawn and staggered off home. This North African life produces highs like no others—highs brought on by the food, drink, the desert and the beach, and ceaseless mingling with the polyglot, multicultural population. The place is crammed with eccentrics and artists who have one thing in common—they're all hooked on Tangier. It's a writer's paradise, especially a young writer. After a while the city gets a hold on you, and you don't want to leave for any reason.

September 19 - Marrakesh

Villa Gazebo is rented to Sanche[2] and Nancy de Gramont. I've shaved my head again. I feel comfortable in Moroccan robes. I'm reading a tragedy a day. Greek.

September 25 - Dar Tounsi

No rain for two years. A chicken will run after the stone you have thrown to drive it away. At four o'clock in the

1. Brion Gysin's Moroccan friend and factotum.
2. a.k.a. Ted Morgan: French/American author of *Literary Outlaw: The Life and Times of William S. Burroughs*; *Lives to Give*; *Rowing toward Eden*; *An Uncertain Hour*; *Maugham*; *FDR*; *Churchill: Young Man in a Hurry 1874-1915*; *Wilderness at Dawn*, and other books.

afternoon, when the heat is at its greatest, the dust sucked from the earth envelopes whole groves of palms, then moves on, a solid wall blanking out the mountains. Dust boils away from a mule's feet. The wind rasps in the palm fronds as dry dates rattle to earth.

This afternoon I stalked and killed an adder that had slithered up the grape arbor.

October 2

A fat Moroccan in a faded blue robe is sound asleep on the bench of a small café. He sleeps with his mouth open and the flies walking on his face are exploring the inside of his mouth. Is he dead or asleep? He opens one eye and spits out the flies trapped in his mouth.

TRIP TO SEGUIA EL HAMRA AND RIO DE ORO
(SPANISH SAHARA)

October 15

Port of Las Palmas: old, vertical prowed ships and ocean-going tug boats are anchored in the distance, Japanese whalers lie in dry dock. Korean trawlers (Inchon), incredibly filthy Spanish freighters, oil slicks with wooden boards, egg crates and life jackets rising and falling in the scummy swell. Rotten fishing boats encrusted with fish scales, ice houses; old, blond, tanned Swedes offering tours of the harbour, tapa bars serving beer, cheap cigarettes and cheap whiskey. Spanish port people: fishermen, stevedores, truckdrivers, painters and fitters, old men with canes sitting on boxes, taxi-drivers, and icemen: all hard, poor, small men with straight mouths and creased eyes reflecting the tragedy of Spain.

October 16 - El Aaiún, Seguia el Hamra

A domed white town with the flat yellow desert stretching

in all directions.

The trumpet blows as the Spanish flag is lowered at dusk. The Spanish Foreign Legion—*El Tercio*—stands at attention as the wind whips in from the desert, then marches smartly away chanting, *"¡Somos los novios de la muerte!"*

October 17

The smell of wind off the desert never varies. It smells of dust and excrement.

October 18 - Smara

Joe and I have visited the mosque and Kasbah which Michel Vieuchange described in his posthumously published *Smara: The Forbidden City*. The stonework is characteristic of its Saharan builders—sophisticated, delicate, strong. In 1926 Vieuchange made the trip by foot and camel dressed as a Berber woman. The disguise didn't work. He was robbed by his guides and died of dysentery in Agadir.

Tonight we walked out into the desert under a full moon. A slight wind from the north. We climbed a hill for a better view of the town and the surrounding desert. It was spooky out there. To me the land seemed dangerous and inhospitable; for Joe it was beautiful and gentle, because it is so unprotected. Not one shrub, not one bush or cactus grows in this stony land. Polished stones glitter like coins under moonlight. The desert is littered with invaluable and inconvertible treasure; no wonder it encourages mysticism.

October 19 - الصحرا

A truck bumped across the desert as a star fell from the sky and burst over the plain. The moon rose green and round above the earth that seemed flat and disc-shaped.

Our truck jolted to a stop, and the Saharans climbed down and kneeled toward the east. When they got back on board, their foreheads were glazed with sand.

October 23 - Villa Cisneros (Rio de Oro)

Yesterday we lay on top of cast-iron manhole covers for nineteen hours on the back of the truck bringing us here.

The desert was as hard and as flat as a tennis court. It must have been under water once, for shells littered the sand and the stones were round and smooth. I picked up a thousand-year-old oyster shell that will be my paperweight in Tangier. The mirages crowded in, cutting us off from the horizon. These shimmering lakes crept to within a few hundred yards in all directions but windward. Cement markers every two km. guided us through. We traversed what must have been an ancient lava flow where the terrain seems to have exploded. A chaotic landscape, where the stones were porous, the surface cratered and uneven. Hollow boulders looked like the skulls of ancient animals. The carcasses of spiny fish and vertebrae of extinct monsters faced each other in a Mexican standoff. Stalagmites and stalactites, caverns and fissures and mountains of bones. It was a frightening sight, and I was glad to leave it behind.

October 24

Don't expect protection in the desert. The beauty is stark and uncompromising. There is no escaping it. Like the universe it's out there in every direction. You're in a 360° situation. You look at it, and it's looking back at you.

Aboard the Leon y Castillo - *somewhere between Villa Cisneros and La Güera.*

We are comfortably installed on this small steamer heading

south toward the Tropic of Cancer. The African coast is visible to port—a low, white line of sandy cliffs where the Sahara meets the Atlantic. The world's biggest goddamn beach, as Brion says. I think Gericault's *Medusa* went down around here somewhere. I have thrown overboard an empty Fundador bottle with a note in it. The note reads: "Someone help me! I'm a prisoner! I am re-reading *The Naked Lunch*. (signed) J. Hopkins, somewhere off Saharan Africa, October 25, 1967."

October 27 - La Güera, on the frontier with Mauritania

Heads of *chuchos* and unknown fish with large teeth litter this beach at La Güera. Buoys strain on ropes in milky green water. This is a typical 19th-century Saharan African port town off the main shipping lines. Way, way off. Old steamer offshore, puff of black smoke from the straight stack, waiting while the launch unloads cargo.

Standing knee deep in the water, black stevedores take the crates and barrels on their shoulders and pile the stuff on the beach. The languid pace of unloading. Some children in swimming (their black heads dot the milky green water). On the point sit the crumbling stone foundations of an ancient fish factory. Smell of dogfish drying in the sun. The water teems with gray stinging bottom fish; sharks lurk offshore where waves break in slow motion. A dangerous place to swim.

A half mile inland the town is visible: a low, haphazard grouping of structures. The yellow and red flag, signifying Spanish military presence, snaps in the wind. Travel inland is a dangerous business. Sandstorms are common. Rasping at high speed over the rough surface of the desert, they produce enough static electricity to make the hair on your head stand straight up.

A few blacks lying on the beach observe the unloading. They keep an eye on the American travellers, swimming and sunning while they wait to leave this desolate place, wondering whatever made them come here in the first place.

October 29 - El Aaiún (The Springs)

View from the bar La Unión across the concrete park, the empty concrete benches, the lines of concrete tiles converging on infinity, the geometric whitewashed and tan-washed houses with snow-white domes that vanish down empty streets: a kind of M.C. Escher maze that would look the same turned upside down. It is three o'clock in the afternoon. Telephone wires tangle under the brilliant yellow sun, under a brilliant blue sky. Whining Arab music oozes like hot oil through the dusty silence. A solitary Spanish legionnaire slumps before his beer. The wind whips along a swirl of dirt and paper. A street ends, open. Across the dry river bed where water has not flowed for hundreds of years, a peaked dune of sand formed by a jagged ridge casts a sawblade shadow.

This is the Sahara. We took pictures of each other in this empty square at this hour because the light was good and because this one-horse town with nobody but us in it seemed to embody the spirit of the trip.

November 3 - Chez Milhet, Casablanca

Dirty, dusty, exhausted and elated, we steamed in from the desert at dawn to find our favourite restaurant open. The best-tasting eggs, bacon, coffee, toast and brandy in the world, followed by more coffee, more brandy, cigarettes and sleep.

November 4 - back in Marrakesh

Why does Paul live in Tangier? Because it is poised between the timeless civilization of the Mediterranean and the eternal nothingness of the Sahara. This kind of balance appeals to him.

November 6

Yesterday Bill Willis[1] took me to the Mamounia to introduce me to Paul Getty who is building a house here.

November 21

Letter from Brion: *As usual, I hardly know what I'm doing. Hamdulilla! For that reason I have put off and put off my trip to Paris where I don't want to go, as you know.*

Like many another in Tanja at the moment, I have broken out in spots. How have your healths been on that trip? I've been to a great wedding in the mountains and made tapes of Jebala.[2] Did you collect music in Rio de Oro and how was the security? Will people be suspicious of my UHER tape-recorder? They were in Jebel Habib near here. I am still longing to hear precise details about money and transport.

I miss you both here in Tangier and will try to make it to Marrakesh when I get back. But will you still be there?

November 22

Targuisti's tale: "One night Brion had to go to Casablanca. Nobody could talk him out of it. So we got on his motorcycle—it was well past midnight—and rode all night through the fog. We arrived after dawn. In a café he looked at me and said, 'What are we doing here? Why did you let me come?' Every night we smoked kif and had the Jilala in, every night."

November 28

Brion is many-sided, like a prism. *Shira* brings out the despair and the conviction that the planet is going to hell. What matters is to get off it as soon as possible. "What is

1. An American architect living in Marrakesh. He designed the Getty home and many others, incorporating Moroccan craftsmanship and architectural detail into his designs.
2. Mountain music.

more important than sex?" he asks in desperation. "What else matters?

"All my life I've been waiting and waiting. What am I waiting for?

"I'm telling you, man, they're just the worst possible hangup." (women) "I'm scared of these people. All my life I've been avoiding them."

This is *shira* talking.

December 2

Why did Brion try to kill Hamri?[1] Targuisti had to drag him off. He was raving, out of his mind. Was it love, or what? Brion has a fear of being poisoned by some woman, namely Jane Bowles. Targuisti remarked on his strength: it was like wrestling with a man in a Jilala trance who wants to do injury to himself, like fighting ten men. There was a great trembling force in the limbs. And then, when he was subdued (B's eyes can be wild—T. remarked on this), a tumble of words, oaths, accusations, the whole history of their relationship. Hamri crouched in the corner, terrified.

December 31

To finish the year I'll quote from Camus:

"In order to speak about all and to all, one has to speak of what all know and of the reality common to us all. The sun, rains, necessity, desire, the struggle against death—these are the things that unite us all."

Resistance, Rebellion, and Death.

1. Moroccan painter from the village of Jajouka.

1968

Don't know what they lace the *majoun* with down here. Last night Paul and Talitha Getty threw a New Year's Eve party at their palace in the Medina. Ira, Joe and I went to meet the Beatles. John Lennon and Paul McCartney were there, flat on their backs. They couldn't get off the floor let alone talk. I've never seen so many people out of control.

We have a New Year and a brilliant day. A blizzard swept the High Atlas during the night, covering the mountains with snow right down to the level of the hot dusty plain. Here in Morocco we lead the most amazing lives: one foot in the nineteenth century, the other in the twentieth. Luxury and austerity go hand in hand. The raw beauty of the place never ceases to amaze me.

Our time is drawing to a close here; Joe and I look forward to going to New York. As usual, we place great hopes in America. I'm already beginning to make notes for the next book.

January 7 - Tangier

Before leaving for New York, we stopped in on Paul to say goodbye and found him huddled in the corner, his face rippled with worry.

"She's spent all my money!" he moaned, pointing at the floor toward Jane's flat. "She's gone crazy!"

Jane, he told us, had moved to the Hotel Atlas and spent every day at the Parade, handing out money and drinks to every lush in Tangier. She had gone through Paul's bank account in a matter of days. Then she prostrated herself on the floor of the American Consulate, refusing to move until Frances Dixon[1] gave her a drink.

"Talk to her," Paul pleaded. "Do something!"

We went downstairs. Instead of the basketcase we had been expecting, we found Jane dolled up as if she were going to a party. Completely manic, she was pacing the floor sipping a highball. I'd never seen her touch a drop of alcohol before. What with all the medicine she takes, booze is strictly proscribed. She was cracking jokes in English, Spanish and Arabic. Her entourage of women were rolling on the floor like a herd of seals bellowing with laughter. The odd thing was that she seemed completely sane—drunk, yes, but bursting with life and humour. Paul seemed to be the neurotic one, helpless, with the strength drained out of him, worried about money and not knowing how to control his wife.

(What we didn't realise at the time was that this was Jane's last hurrah. A few days later Paul took her to a sanatorium in Spain, and she hasn't come back to Tangier. Written July 28.)

February 3 - Hotel Chelsea, New York

Three framed Brion Gysin desert paintings decorate my wall. They mesmerize me. Brion says this is the way every planet in the solar system looks. In two, the land is indistinguishable from the sky. The sun (or something) is visible in the dusty atmosphere. An infinity of horizontal lines leads to the eternal horizon. A terrain that will never change. Only with the greatest effort can one force oneself to cross it. As Brion says, This is it, this is the desert, this is the universe, this is the past, this is the future, this is us.

---

1. Wife of the U.S. Consul General in Tangier.

Here in snowy New York these paintings inspire me with visions for a desert novel.

Tennessee Williams' short stories: his sympathy for his characters' weaknesses. He dwells on failure to demonstrate his understanding of the human condition.

February 13

Letter from P.B.

You ask about my summer plans. At the moment there are none, although Jane's health could conceivably invent something by then, I suppose. I feel sure I shall be here or hereabouts. Who wants to be elsewhere? . . . Really nothing happens in Tangier, or, at least, nothing that I am aware of.

M'rabet went yesterday to a saint's tomb somewhere near Ksar el Kebir, returning today in a happy state. He now believes the tseuheur *which he suspected someone had made against him has been annulled, so we can rest in peace for a few days, maybe.*

The weather has been clear and warm up until two days ago, when clouds gathered in answer to the rain-prayers that were being led by the fqihs *all over town. It poured all night, and managed to flood the streets. There are still lakes here and there, and the frogs suddenly became very vocal under my windows. Unfortunately I can't record them, as all my tape-recorders are out of commission.*

February 15 - Hotel Chelsea, NYC

Letter from Brion Gysin in Tangier:

. . . The weather is beautiful but the town seems emptier every day. . . . Jane wasn't the only nutcase who rang the bell or hammered at the bathroom window. . . . M'rabet got married last week but Paul doesn't know about that yet. Targuisti dixit. I can only tell you that January has been a jewel. I got some good recordings of 60 or more little kids praying for rain and it's like

Joe McPhillips, John Hopkins and the "White Nile", Nairobi, Kenya, 1961. Photograph for *The East African Standard*.

"Literary Tangier". Standing: John Hopkins; front row, l-r: Omar Pound, Joe McPhillips, Emilio Sanz, Jane Bowles, Christopher Wanklyn, William Burroughs, Paul Bowles. Tangier 1963. © Robert Freson.

Jane Bowles in Asilah, 1963. © Robert Freson.

Paul Bowles and John Hopkins, Sidi Kacem, Tangier, 1972.
© Abdelouhid Boulaich.

Tennessee Williams and Ellen Ann Ragsdale, Tangier, 1973.
© Tessa Codrington.

John Hopkins in Moroccan Sahara, 1974.
© Brahim ben Abdelrahman.

Ellen Ann Ragsdale in Tangier, 1973.
© Tessa Codrington.

Jim Wyllie at Zero, Place de la Kasbah, Tangier, 1975.
© Tessa Codrington.

Ellen Ann Ragsdale and the Hon. David Herbert arriving
at St. Andrew's Church, Tangier, June 25, 1979.
© Dfuf.

Brion Gysin and his four-toed foot, from the Bandaged Poet Series, Amsterdam, One World Poetry Festival, 1979. © Ira Cohen.

Mohammed M'rabet and Paul Bowles, Tangier.
©Cherie Nutting.

a summer day outside, right now.

February 20 - New York

Working every day in this crazy hotel making notes for my next novel, *Tangier Buzzless Flies,* inspired by 1. the desert trip to Spanish Sahara, 2. an article I read about tetanus in *Scientific American*, and 3. my affection for Tangier.

March 28 - Back in Tangier

The sheer glory and joy of being alive that one feels in this town. This must come across in the novel. My hero comes here, not to indulge himself, but to be cured of death.

April 1

After dinner at Marguerite McBey's, Paul and I dropped in on Alfred Chester[1] in his house at the bottom of the Old Mountain Road. An enormous baby, he must be treated like one to be happy. Otherwise, he pouts. Several dogs sleep in the same bed with him. The place stank of dog piss. One room was shoulder deep with firewood, another housed a mountain of oranges that looked as though they had been delivered by dump truck. A drunken fat woman with red hair who Alfred called "the living end" lounged by the fire. A Moroccan boy asked if we wanted tea or orange juice. Alfred started taking off his clothes in front of the roaring fire. (The wall above the fireplace had been blackened by flames.) "Why don't you stay?" he shrieked. "Why are you going? Will you come back?" He followed us into the wintry night in his underwear. Fat blubbery hairless flesh. "Of course you won't come back!" he screamed, "You're snobs! You hate us!" Then

1. American writer living in Tangier; author of *The Exquisite Corpse*; *Jamie Is my Heart's Desire*, and other books.

he whimpered, "Just say so—will you come back?"

May 7

Tangier, the white city poised atop the dark continent which turns out to be the continent of light.

June 1

The Moroccans say to kill one fly in winter is the same as killing a thousand in summer.

June 3

The Attempt published by Secker & Warburg in London. A reviewer called it "A hitchhiker's guide to Peru."

June 4 - Marrakesh

Madman on the glittering road. He jumped from the shadow of a tree where he had been lying invisible in the midday glare. Bellowing, gesticulating, he ran toward me. The eyes were all whites, there was slobber on his jaw. Through the rents in his ragged djellaba the body was visible—fish-belly white. Arms and face had been roasted black by the sun. A huge man, massive, barefoot. Screaming, he came closer—a stiff halting run. He bared his teeth and ran right by. He did not see me. He sees nothing but his own visions.

June 5

Robert Kennedy shot in California. Those bastards.

June 6

R.K. dead. Kennedy King Kennedy. Who's next?

June 8

Marrakesh is like an immersion tank. I do not feel the air.

Its temperature is the same as my own. There is no resistance, no sensation of air. You want to take off your clothes, as I have just done, to expose the skin. The power of the sun is ferocious, the temperature is over 100°F, but in the shade I do not sweat. I am neither hot nor cold. A slight breeze enters the open window; I feel perfectly at one with the atmosphere.

June 9 - مراكش

The silence of noonday heat. The sun pouring out of the white-hot sky flattens the earth. Nothing moves, not birds or dogs or humans. I lie on a bench in this small, low room and look at the ceiling. Geckoes poke their heads between the hairy palm beams and peer at me with agate eyes. On the other side of the courtyard someone has turned on a radio. The nasal wail of Arab music slithers like a cobra through the heat and silence. The news comes on. A hoarse voice speaks rapidly in Arabic.

June 10

Marrakesh spring. Red poppies among the green wheat. Storks. Killed another snake on the path last night. A bad one—black.

June 29 - Marrakesh

A mean wind blows this time of year. They call it the Shergui because it comes from the east. It may blow for a day or a week, and there's no good in it. It's hot, like a blast from flames, and as long as it blows the heat remains constant, night and day.

Today was the worst. Moaning around the corners of the house, the wind woke me before dawn, and it blew hard all morning. The sky was opaque and coloured orange with flying sand. The grit penetrated everywhere—the ears, the nose—I could taste it between my teeth.

I drove to the Djemaa el Fna to have my head shaved. Outside the barber shop, a group of Mauritanian musicians was sitting on the pavement. The blowing sand had sewed orange-coloured seams into the folds of their indigo robes.

All of a sudden there was a shout and the music stopped, followed by a chorus of wails. The musicians got to their feet and were pointing into the wind. A woman fell to her knees, her eyes rolling.

"God save us!" she screamed, and, "Agadir! Agadir!" (In 1961 Agadir was destroyed by an earthquake.)

We ran outside as a pink and orange cloud, which must have been a mile high and which covered the plain from horizon to horizon, advanced upon Marrakesh like a colossal churning wave or rolling wall. Everything in its path, including the Koutoubia minaret, was swallowed and lost from view and apparently obliterated forever. There was no point in running nor time to think: in less than a minute it was upon us.

The wind abruptly dropped, and we were engulfed in a mist of swirling dust. Voices became muffled and vision vague. The dust, which was as fine as talcum powder, was falling like snow, and the silence was not unlike the hush that accompanies a snowstorm. The world was enveloped in a mysterious saffron-coloured light, and the air was still. It was quite peaceful, and those who had been afraid cautiously raised their heads and looked about. Everybody sat quietly and waited, because there was nothing else to do. All shouting had stopped.

The light, meanwhile, was fading fast. The dust was thickening, and the saffron glow darkened to amber. When the sunlight had been shut out altogether, we groped about calling names. It was blacker than the blackest night, so it was safer not to move at all. Someone gripped my arm. It was my friend Mejdubi. I couldn't see him, but I could hear him chuckling. Like all medicine men, he thrived on catastrophes. He had done a big business in Agadir at the time of the earthquake.

We wrapped our turbans around our faces, and for the better part of an hour did not speak. I opened my eyes to an amber glow that had begun to suffuse the mist. Those around us stirred and murmured as though they were waking from a dream. The swirling dust was once more permeated with saffron light.

Then things happened very quickly. The wind began to blow again, and the world and everything in it grew brighter and more distinct. The wind freshened and became colder; the temperature had dropped several degrees. As the sandstorm rolled away, we unwrapped our faces and looked around. The air was clear and I could see all the way to the mountains.

July 14 - Dar Tounsi

Today, in the privacy of my adobe office, I started writing my new novel, *Tangier Buzzless Flies*. Outside it's 110° in the shade. If placed in the sun, a thermometer will explode.

July 20 - Marrakesh

The man with two wives.

Hussein is the leader of a Gnaoua group who brings his musicians to play at my house. The other night he invited me to his home for dinner, where he introduced me to his wives. One was a diminutive, tattooed Berber woman from the Atlas Mountains, as white as any English lady, but oriental-looking nevertheless. The other was a robust Saharan girl from the River Dra, with scars for decorations. During dinner Hussein explained how the women took turns. On alternating nights one or the other prepared his food and shared his bed. The Saharan girl cooked a hot, spicy dish which made me sweat, while the Berber woman apparently used a lot of milk in her recipes. The system must have worked, for they were all happy and smiling. The Berber woman proudly showed me her little white baby, and the Saharan girl was bouncing a brown one on her knee. They both wanted to know how many wives and children I had. I confessed I didn't have any, bringing the conversation to a stop. Hussein came to my defense by pointing out that a young man likes to enjoy his freedom before settling down. On that there was general agreement.

July 25 - Casablanca

The train ride from Marrakesh to Casablanca: My excitement mixed with nostalgia as the train chugged forth from the Marrakesh railroad station, more French than Moroccan with its manicured trees, dripping fountain and red wall. All the windows were open, and a German seated across from me in the compartment was speechless from the heat. We rode out into a hot blast of desert air. Why did that heat, the arid landscape, and the diminutive African railroad stations we passed one after another define my existence and convince me that without doubt I was living at a precise time and place? The heat did it—heat set up a resistance that made the train ride memorable.

An alert was passed from car to car to shut the windows. A sandstorm was approaching. The sky turned rose, and grit hissed against the glass. I thought the German was going to faint. Then the air cleared, and we could open the windows once more. The sun was poised on the horizon like a molten plum. We were leaving the plain of the Houz, and the air suddenly became much cooler, the first real freshness I have felt in days. How can I explain what that drop in temperature made me feel? Not relief particularly—in Mogador there is the sea and Marrakesh evenings are balmy—but I was grateful for change and the possibility of movement. I shall always be.

The streets of Casablanca—cool, spacious, already quiet at the time of my arrival. Leaving my suitcase at the Hotel Astoria and walking to Chez Milhet, I was consumed by a confidence that freedom brings—of feeling at home in the half-deserted streets of this North African city, where prostitutes beckon from doorways, of being happy alone, of sensing who I am and what I respond to and what means nothing.

Today I have seen the mud dwellings on the hot plain, the stacks of threshed wheat, the animals going in circles on the threshing floor, the little animals on the inside where they don't have to walk so far, the children waving and running after the train. I was moved by the unspoken openness and glory of the plain. I don't have to look into their houses or examine their lives: I know that that landscape and the Moroccans in it represent something totally human, something harmoniously timeless to which I give my full allegiance. The heat did it, and gratitude for coolness as the sun slipped behind the mounting horizon. The old wooden train, trundling along with the windows wide open, filled my heart with joy.

Tomorrow I fly to Spain to find Jane.

July 27 - Malaga

A nun led me up the path through the garden to the sanatorium known as La Clínica de Reposo de los Angeles. It was nearing lunchtime and the ladies were sitting on the front porch, chattering to each other. My eyes went among them and picked out Jane sitting silent and alone on a bench in the back. The nun helped her to her feet. I kissed her, and she said: "What are you doing here?" Two hours later I went away from that place. The life had been crushed out of her by drugs and by disease. There was no spirit left. She said she would never leave the Clínica where one day could be no different from another. The nuns said she did not wish to leave her room. She was ashamed of her shaggy appearance and told me not to ask other friends in Tangier to visit.

August 17 - Dar Tounsi

My landlords here in the palmeraie are Ganya and Ira (*dit* Belline) Bilankine, nephew and niece of Igor Stravinsky. Tall, elegant, her skin permanently bronzed by the North African sun, Ira is invariably dressed in her uniform of light cotton trousers, pastel blouse and silk scarf wrapped around her head. She earns a meagre living selling oranges and olives from the farm. The Moroccans who buy her crop respect her because she is aristocratic and haughty; also because she drives a hard bargain.

From my writer's window I watch Ganya striding through the olive trees, Negrita straining on a leash. Faded blue shirt, brown shorts and canvas shoes. Graying beard. Each day he takes a pill to control epilepsy. Ira: "I took one once to see how strong it was and slept for two days."

Each summer, to escape the infernal Marrakesh heat, Ira and her friend Boul[1] drive in Boul's old Pontiac to Tangier to stay with David Herbert[2] for a month of parties, leaving Ganya behind to look after the farm. Ira worries constantly about her brother when she's away. One night Ganya fought a huge tiger snake for two hours in the dark before the thing slithered from the house. He

1. The Countess de Breteuil, proprietress of the Villa Taylor in Marrakesh.
2. The uncle of the Earl of Pembroke, and long-time resident of Tangier, David made a great many Moroccan friends and was a tireless promoter of Tangier. He was the author of *Second Son* and was the godfather of the author's oldest son. He died in Tangier in 1995.

fearlessly shoos away scorpions and tarantulas. They own ten dogs. Ira collects bones from the back door of the Hotel Mamounia, which she boils to make a soup to feed them. No animals may be killed on their property; the Moroccans must slaughter their sheep elsewhere on the Aid El Kebir.

Ira refers to Ganya in the following manner: "Oh, he is listening to the radio—the eight o'clock news, or he's fixing the *moteur*, or he's reading or making coffee, or repairing this or that. . . . " All manly pursuits that are his domain. Ira likes to pretend her brother is the man of the house, but she is the responsible one. All her life she has had to work to support the useless men in her life.

The family owned a sugar beet plantation and distillery in the Ukraine. Ira remembers that, in 1914, to keep the vodka from falling into the hands of the advancing German army, the vats were emptied into the river, and the dead fish floated to the surface. The family emigrated to France and opened a restaurant in Biarritz. At fifteen Ira was hired as a shop assistant by Chanel. Her father, an admiral in the Czarist navy, never did a stroke of work after they left Russia. Later she became a set designer for Louis Jouvet in Paris. During the war they hid from the Nazis in a villa outside Marseilles. In 1946 she came to Morocco with two Americans, Jay Hazelwood and Bill Chase, and founded the Parade Bar, Tangier's premier watering hole.

To make ends meet, Ira opened a flower shop in Tangier and sold antiques until David Herbert got her a job as a housekeeper for Barbara Hutton. When the onset of middle-aged asthma made Ira's life in Tangier unbearable, BH bought her this farm in the palm groves outside Marrakesh: forty acres of olive and citrus with a simple but elegant adobe house built, I am told, by the Tolstoy family.

Every Saturday night Ira and Ganya climb into the old 2CV they call "Doushka" and go to the movies, no matter what's on. Ira wears her baggy Saharan trousers—gift from a Foreign Legion officer she had an affair with back in the '30s. Ganya wears his only suit—wool, three piece, wide lapels, made in Paris before the war. When she arranges his tie, he makes a face at me over her shoulder, as if to say, "Ugh. Women's stuff."

About once a week I walk through the olive groves to their house for lunch or dinner. (In Marrakesh one lunches outside during winter, inside in summer because of the heat.) The meal is simple, often vegetarian because meat is expensive. No alcohol for Ganya, no peppery food. His tough, calloused hands are thick with eczema. Dirt under the nails. The Moroccans know he is not like other people. He talks to animals and to himself; for this they respect him.

Each has his own dog, Cleopatra and Negrita, and during the meal they invariably fight under the table. While Ganya was clearing away, Ira confided, "I only hope he dies before me. What would happen to him on his own? Look at him. He's sixty, but he has the figure of a young man."

After dinner Ganya and I walked to the pump. "You know, dear John," he said, "I am not right in the head. I must take pills." He puffed on his pipe. The moon was so bright you could have read a newspaper by it. "It has always been so. She worries about me. She's afraid of what will happen to me if she dies first. She is growing older quicker than me. What would I do? That is a very good question, my dear John. What would I do?" His words were drowned out by a chorus of frogs.

This brother and sister act is typical of the kind of eccentric characters you find in Morocco. This hospitable North African kingdom welcomes refugees, misfits, artists and adventurers from the four corners of the earth. They bring with them remnants of cultures that no longer exist and recreate them here. We have a bit of old Russia right here in the palmeraie.

August 29

As electricity has not yet come to the oasis, the only place to keep things cool is in my old-fashioned icebox, which means I have to drive to Marrakesh every day for a block of ice. The ice is produced at the Flag brewery in the industrial quarter and distributed through a small hole in a mud wall. There is always a mob of mainly Moroccan women waiting in the blazing heat, and invariably a struggle ensues when the ice starts to come out. You have to have the right change and be prepared to defend yourself against ladies who will pinch, scratch, and call you every name in the book. Today was the worst. I came away with my prized block of ice but lost one sandal in the melée and my dark glasses were pulled off my face and trampled.

October 28

A letter from Robert Hemenway at *The New Yorker*, accepting my short story (first chapter of the novel) *Tangier Buzzless Flies*. Yahoo!

December 5

Reading Pound's *Cantos*—a canto a day. From Canto LIV: "Emptiness is the beginning of all things."

1969

March 1 - طنجة

I was on the bus, one of the sky-blue Volvos recently imported by the R.A.T.T. (*Régie Anonyme des Transports Tangerois*) to replace the ageing fleet of brown and yellow Renaults.

Like a block of ice hewn from a Scandinavian glacier, the bus was inching through Dradeb, one of the city's poorest *barrios*, known to foreign residents as "Suicide Village." It was market day, and the bus was pushing its way through a human moraine of Moroccans intent on getting their shopping done before the day stoked up. From his blackened cave a grimy charcoal vendor blinked like a mole into the morning light. A weathered fisherman hawked fresh sardines with piercing, guttural cries that seemed to echo the harshness of his life. Fresh-faced country girls in floppy straw hats and red-and-white-striped shawls sat primly before shiny piles of home-grown vegetables. The shouting and the haggling, the flies and the confusion, the sickly-sweet smell of uncollected garbage: it was a scene to send tourists home in strait-jackets.

Beneath the relentless North African sun, the bus's cool blue hue had already begun to fade. Overcrowding, the dents from countless accidents, and shoddy maintenance had taken their toll. The ice cube was beginning to look decidedly lumpy. The new uniform issued to the driver had already worn out. The man at the wheel looked more at home in his embroidered skull cap, striped summer djellaba, and pointed yellow slippers.

At the place where the road crosses Jew's River—a parched gully most of the year; a dangerous and destructive current during the rainy season—the bus lurched to a stop. The passengers crowded to the windows: an accident had occurred. Trailing the black tail of a skid mark, a motorbike lay on the pavement. A boy with a bloody arm was sitting beside it. Jammed up against the curb near the corner of the bridge was a white Volkswagen beetle with a Gibraltar licence plate. It looked as though the car swerved to avoid the oncoming motorcycle which nevertheless crashed straight into it.

"Suicide Village" was living up to its name!

I recognized the VW instantly. It was driven by Madeleine van Breugel, a Dutch girl who had come to Tangier with her one-year-old daughter visiting friends. Her husband, a veterinary surgeon, was in Kenya.

Looking down from the bus window directly above the car, I couldn't see her face; only her red-tipped fingers were visible gripping the wheel. The knuckles were white. The Moroccans were pressing so densely around the car that she couldn't open the door.

Jumping down from the bus, I pushed my way through the crowd and tapped on the car window. The tense expression on her face instantly transformed into one of relief. I went to the boy and found he was not seriously hurt. We took him to the local dispensary and had his arm bandaged. Madeleine, who I had thought a rather cold fish when I met her, suddenly turned talkative and passionate. For rescuing her from the hooded Moors she thanked me with hugs and kisses.

March 11

Finished the first draft of *Tangier Buzzless Flies*. Freedom!

May 20 - Tangier

Having received a barrage of love letters from me, Madeleine has left her daughter and husband in Holland and returned alone to Tangier. Tall (5'9"), with grayish-green eyes, erect posture and long auburn hair, her presence in Tangier has created a stir. Some people are fascinated by her aristocratic beauty; others are put off by her haughty manner.

May 25

McPhillips has done it again. The American School production of Euripides' *The Bacchae*: music by Paul Bowles, make-up by Brion Gysin, costumes by Yves St. Laurent, chorus led by Pam Weston, Randy's[1] daughter. My contribution was the set consisting of gigantic handmade baskets. Dubbed "Moroccan rocket ships," some four meters high, simulating the towers of Thebes, these massive flexible pillars can be made to shake and heave during the earthquake scene.

September 13 - Tangier

Two months ago exactly, on July 13, Brion Gysin and I were involved in a freak motorcycle accident in which he was seriously injured while the White Nile and I escaped unscathed. The incident stirred up a controversy in Tangier. I have been accused of driving carelessly, injuring my friend and being indifferent to his welfare; others have blamed Brion for whipping up the hysteria by blabbing accusations and half-truths all over town.

In order to set the record straight, I want to write down exactly what happened: a description of events as I experienced them.

On July 13 the *poniente*, or west wind, brought to Tangier

---

1. The jazz pianist Randy Weston.

one of those warm, limpid days that make you want to drop everything and run for the beach. I motorcycled south and picnicked with Nancy and Sanche de Gramont and their children near Asilah. (Sanche later told me that Nancy had woken up that morning with the premonition that something awful was about to happen to Brion.)

After lunch and a swim I rode the White Nile back to Tangier and parked outside Brion's apartment at 59, Moussa Ben Noussair. The brilliant day had put him into an expansive mood, and we decided to drive out to the Caves of Hercules for a swim and supper.

Brion's right shoulder is imprinted with a blue star-burst tattoo. He learned long-distance swimming in Canada. The trick is to let the arm flop limply on the surface before a slow, easy pull through the water. That way the arm muscles stay loose, and little energy is expended. I swam for a mile or so in the easy swell off the Atlantic.

Afterwards we dined on grilled swordfish and went through a bottle of Jack Daniels at the restaurant atop the Caves. Brion was in full song, making connections and inspiring me with ideas for my novel, *Tangier Buzzless Flies*. After dinner, he talked about Hemingway. "You may not like his writing, but you have to respect his accomplishment, and he did it without any help from his friends." Meaning: Brion has been down on his luck lately. His funds are low, and he has been depressed by the poor sales of his book, *The Process*. His best friend (Burroughs) and patrons (the Heidsick family) are far away and apparently indifferent to his plight.

We were about to hop aboard the bike when Brion whispered that he had just spotted Princess Ruspoli[1] getting out of a car in front of the restaurant. This woman inspires

1. A French woman née de Chambrun and direct descendant of the Marquis de Lafayette; author of *Le Retour du Phoenix* and *L'Epervier Divin*.

a kind of dread in Brion. He calls her a witch and avoided her on the stairs when she came to visit Jane Bowles, whose flat was next door to his when he lived at Immueble Itesa.

The weather had changed while we were in the restaurant. Instead of the gentle *poniente* pushing from behind, we drove into the teeth of the *levante*. The gusting wind buffeted the White Nile, and I had to grip the handlebars with all my strength to keep the machine from being blown off the road.

We were zipping along the airport road opposite the textile factory when an ancient truck appeared over the rise ahead. I could tell it was old by the dimness of its lights. The movement of those pale orbs told me the driver was having difficulty steering his decrepit vehicle in the gale, and I manoeuvred my machine to the very edge of the road to avoid a collision.

When the truck passed, there was a loud click. I felt nothing; there had been no jolt or shock of contact; the BMW purred on through the cool night like the Titanic after it had grazed the iceberg.

"Brion!" I shouted. "Are you all right?"

His reply: "I think I just lost my left foot!"

Incredulous, I slammed on the brakes.

"Keep going!" he screamed. "Drive to the lights of the city!"

I hit the gas and we accelerated toward Tangier. How was it possible for his foot to have been injured? This is the question I keep asking myself to this day. His feet were tucked in behind mine; both were protected by the horizontally opposed cylinders of the BMW.

I stopped the bike beneath the first street light in Tangier and was appalled by what I saw. Brion's desert boot was filled to the ankle with blood. Blood was pouring over the top and leaking through the lace holes.

We quickly discussed what to do. As Brion had a horror

of hospitals, we raced up to Dr. Anderson's clínica on the Marshan.

The clínica was dark and the gate locked. Leaving Brion sitting on the curb beneath a street light, I scaled the garden wall, picked my way through the barbed wire and broken glass, and dropped to the other side.

Dr. Anderson came immediately. We helped Brion into the clinica and lay him on the operating table. I couldn't look while Dr. A. cut away the desert boot. Afterwards he told me that his first impression was that Brion had been hit across the top of his foot with an axe.

Dr. A. bandaged the foot and drove us to the Spanish Hospital, where Brion was put into bed and given pain killers. The last thing he said was, "Marta Ruspoli did this to me. She was standing in front of the restaurant and gave me the evil eye."

Fortunately Dr. Alberto, a reputable Spanish surgeon, happened to be in residence. He showed us the X-rays the next morning. Three of Brion's toe bones had been crushed in the accident. They could only be repaired by surgery. Brion moaned about money; I volunteered to pay all his medical expenses. That afternoon Dr. Alberto operated, removing one toe and repairing the others. He assured Brion that once he was back on his feet the loss of his middle toe would not impede his walking.

A week later Brion went home on crutches, his foot in a cast. I paid the surgeon's fee and the hospital bill. On August 6 I flew to Amsterdam for my rendezvous with Madeleine.

On August 30 I returned to Tangier to find a letter from Bill Burroughs waiting for me. In it he accused me of having damaged Brion's literary career. Brion, he claimed, was a "peripatetic" writer; that is, he needed to get up from his desk and walk around for the ideas to flow. As he was now incapable of walking (and therefore of writing) he was deprived of the means of making his living. Being the party responsible for Brion's injury, I should feel obliged to pay a heavy compensation.

I went straight to Brion's and found him at home with Salah, Targuisti and his friend Felicity Mason. He had his foot up. He was in a friendly mood, and wanted to know if I'd seen the van Goghs in Otterloo. When I mentioned Bill's letter he laughed. I went home wondering what the fuss was all about.

The next morning I received an urgent call from Targuisti at Café Pilo. He said Brion needed to talk to me right away. I found him sitting with T. looking very glum. Yesterday's welcoming façade had disappeared. When I sat down he pulled a hundred dollar bill from his pocket and waved it angrily in my face.

"This is all I've got!" he shouted. "There's nothing else left!"

He was trembling all over. Tears were pouring down his face.

"Let's not talk here," I said. "This is not the place."

Targuisti agreed. We hailed a taxi and rode to his apartment building. The tiny elevator would only hold two people, and I got in with Brion. As soon as the elevator started to rise, he tried to pummel me with his crutches. Fortunately the lift was so cramped he couldn't land a blow. Targuisti and I managed to get him into his apartment. He threatened to sue me and claimed he had already consulted a lawyer. I knew he was bluffing. Brion hated lawyers; he had told me he wouldn't go near one if his life depended on it. Nevertheless, it was distressing to see my friend in such a state. I felt responsible but was in a quandary over what to do about it.

This state of affairs lasted several days, with Brion ringing at all hours of the day and night threatening legal action. Finally our mutual friend Marguerite McBey intervened.

She asked an insurance agent named Mr. Raida to help us settle our differences.

Brion and I agreed to see the man and to abide by his decision. We went together to an office on Calle Victor Hugo. Mr. Raida asked us to describe the accident, the resulting injury, the hospitalization, the surgery, the current state of Brion's health, and so forth.

Mr. Raida explained that in cases of this kind the aggrieved party may claim, under French law, *le prix doleur* or "price of pain" which varied according to the seriousness of the injury and any resulting disability.

He read us the list of "prices." Loss of both arms and legs: the *pretium doloris* was $1,000,000! My heart jumped to my throat. I looked apprehensively at Brion; he was sitting on the edge of his chair. Mr. Raida: Loss of both arms, both legs, or an arm and a leg: $500,000! Brion's eyes grew big; his injury, he imagined, was going to make him an instant millionaire! Mr. Raida read on. Loss of a hand, part of one leg, fingers, ears, eyes, and so forth until he found, at the bottom of the list, the loss of the middle toe: $1,500 or 7,500 Moroccan dirhams.

The mention of this comparatively paltry but legally established sum brought Brion to his senses. His injury was not the end of the world. He signed (I have a copy of the document in front of me), accepting the agreed amount and releasing me from further indemnity. I gave him a lift home. In the car he repeated his conviction that Marta Ruspoli had caused the accident. She had given us the evil eye as we drove off on the motorcycle.

[John Hopkins spent the next seven months with Madeleine van Breugel in New York, where he completed the final draft of his novel *Tangier Buzzless Flies*. In February 1970 they made an extensive trip through Guatemala.]

1970

The Attempt, translated by Pauline Petit de la Villeon, has been published as *L'Arpenteur* by Gallimard in Paris.

April 11

Tangier Tales.

Jim Wyllie was walking home through the Kasbah one night when a hooded Moor grabbed him from behind, pressed a knife to his jugular and hissed, "Your money or your life!"

When Jim cheerfully rebuked him in Arabic, the would-be assassin stepped back, replying meekly, "Oh, it's you, Mr. Wyllie. You may pass." Jim went on his way, and the assassin returned to the shadows to await his next victim.

April 20

Josephine Baker is in town. Last night she performed at the Mauritania theatre to raise money for her tribe of orphans. We went with David Herbert, an old friend of hers. Afterwards we crossed the street to the Parade for supper and to listen to her and David reminisce about Paris.

June 23

Madeleine has smuggled a miniature green parrot back from Guatemala. "Chita" sits on her head or nestles under her hair. The two are constant companions. Madeleine's first love is animals, then us.

July 11

Christopher Gibbs[1] and I are the only non-Muslims I know who shave their heads. We laugh at each other's egg-like pates when we run into each other at the Parade.

July 15 - Dar Tounsi

Each morning before putting on my *baboushes*, I give them a good shake in case a scorpion has taken up residence inside.

October 11 - New York

I got off the subway at Brooklyn Heights and bought a copy of *The New Yorker* at the newsstand to discover my story *Tangier Buzzless Flies* on p. 40. Clutching the thing proudly to my chest, I walked whistling to Oliver Smith's (Paul's cousin) house on Willow St. where I'm staying.

October 19

Tangier Buzzless Flies (the novel) has been accepted by Richard Kluger at Atheneum! He has written me a five-page letter about the book which I have spent hours poring over. He wants changes, for the most part good ones.

November 11 - Marrakesh

Boul de Breteuil has given me a room at Villa Taylor where I have plugged in my electric typewriter and started work on another South American novel, *The Flight of the Pelican*.

Villa Taylor is one of the most spectacular houses in Morocco. Built ca. 1923 by the Taylor family who came to Morocco on their steam yacht from Newport, Rhode Island, this mud castle sits in fifteen acres of lush cactus,

---

1. English antique dealer and frequent visitor to Morocco. He built a house in the Ourika valley near Marrakesh.

olive, and palm gardens in the middle of Gueliz. Three hundred artisans from Fez spent a year on the site, adorning the place with painted ceilings, carved plaster friezes, and walls of intricately patterned tiles.

Following the Casablanca Conference in 1943, Winston Churchill and President Roosevelt spent a few days recuperating here. Churchill completed his only wartime drawing at Villa Taylor. When old Mrs. Taylor heard that FDR had spent the night in her house, she refused to set foot in Villa Taylor again.

She sold it to Charles de Breteuil who gave it to his wife as a wedding present. She and her only son Jean live in this enormous house, waited on by a band of devoted servants.

November 22 - Tangier, Lune de miel marocaine

Ana Gabriela's uncle Emile Bonnet (Mr. California ca. 1937) runs the Hotel Atlas in Tangier. A.G. told me about a German couple who came to Morocco on their honeymoon. They went out to a night club where the unsuspecting bridegroom apparently consumed a large quantity of *majoun*. Late that night the hall porter was wakened by blood-curdling screams from above. The terrified Moroccan crept to the door of the bridal suite, where the heavy crashing of furniture persuaded him to call the manager. He was on the phone to Emile when the sound of shattering glass was followed by a glimpse of a naked body hurtling through the air. Fortunately, the German's leap from a second-storey window was broken by a car parked in front of the hotel. The car was a write-off but, miraculously, the German was not seriously injured. Emile arrived and opened the door with a skeleton key. The furniture in the room was smashed to smithereens. He said it looked like the work of a demolition team; everything had been reduced by some gargantuan force to kindling. Cowering in the corner, naked and shivering, was the bride.

The next day, after settling the bill, the honeymooners flew back to Germany.

1971

February 4 - Amsterdam

Living on Kloverniersburgval revising the ms. of *Tangier Buzzless Flies* for Richard Kluger at Atheneum. Madeleine's mother, the Baroness van Nagel, came for tea. She doesn't approve of where we're living; she definitely doesn't approve of me.

March 27 - Tangier

The Schoolmaster's Goat Dance.

Brion Gysin and the painter Hamri threw a party at Jajouka to celebrate the musicians' new clubhouse. Despite torrential rains a crowd from Tangier went—Sanche and Nancy de Gramont, Louise de Meuron, Ahmed Maimouni, and other enthusiasts of mountain music. The invitation was for seven but, as it was Joe's birthday, we sat around Mme. Porte's *salon du thé* drinking dry martinis until nine when we picked up George Staples[1] and headed off into the storm.

George presented Joe with a bottle of Courvoisier which we passed back and forth as the VW's headlights bore a tunnel through the windy night. Branches were down and the road was flooded. By the time we reached Larache the brandy was gone, so we stopped at the Cuatro Caminos truck stop for a bottle of Fundador. At El Ksar el Kebir we turned onto a farm road that led to the hills. The puddles were so deep the water came into the car. At the bottom of Jajouka mountain the other cars were parked: Jeeps,

1. American teacher and writer living in Tangier.

Land Rovers, Toyotas. Deep ruts spoke of these four-wheel-drive vehicles' failure to make it up the hill in the rain.

I was about to park when Joe commanded, "Don't stop here! Gun it!"

I hit the gas and up the goat track we went, sliding in the mud, weaving in and out of boulders. George and Joe got out and pushed and miraculously the old VW, like Herbie the Disney car, kept going up and up. We crested the hill and skated through the mud to the clubhouse. A cheer went up from the Moroccans. How did the battered VW defeat the Jeeps, whose drivers had to trudge uphill in the pouring rain?

After supper the music began. The musicians in their knee-length djellabas and military turbans sat on a stone wall. The rain had stopped but the mud was deep. The voice of the *rhaita*, not unlike the shrill wail of bagpipes, and rattle of drums called the villagers from their huts. Bou Jelloud, a Pan-like figure dressed in hairy goatskins, rushed onto the scene. Steam rose from the hot stinking skins that had just been stripped from a sacrificial animal. This powerful dancer brandished an olive switch. In the midst of his energetic gyrations he made runs at the women, swatting them with the branch. The sexual effect was electric; they screamed and scattered. The symbol was obvious: the goatman had descended from the hills to impregnate the village girls.

After many drinks the schoolmaster tottered from the clubhouse. Recognizing a kindred spirit when he saw one, the goatman beckoned him to join the dance. (Joe's thick curly hair prompted his students in Lima to dub him "*La Oveja*"—the sheep—"*de San Marcos*.") The schoolmaster in his tweed jacket and tie, Bou Jelloud in his smelly, smoking skins: for an hour they danced barefoot in the mud, oblivious to everything but the music.

I remember having more brandies at Cuatro Caminos about 4AM. At five we breakfasted at Café Pilo on *pan tostada* and coffee and hit the hay at dawn.

May 5 - Dar Tounsi

Having laid her husband to rest on San Michele in Venice, Vera Stravinsky has come to Marrakesh to see her cousins. Ira and Ganya went to the Churchill Suite at the Mamounia for dinner; Madeleine and I were invited afterwards. It was like a scene out of Tolstoy: the remains of the meal scattered about the room, the samovar bubbling away while the old Russian ladies sipped neat vodka and summoned up the past.

May 20

Dinner chez Boul at Villa Taylor with Field Marshal Claude Auchinleck. Too hot to sit indoors, we eat in the *riad* waited on by Boul's band of gorgeously costumed servants. A tangerine-coloured hibiscus blossom floats in the marble fountain. The Auk, who once commanded a force of two million men, is now pushing ninety. Stiff as a ramrod and deaf as a post, he lives alone in a little bungalow in Gueliz where, I'm informed, he's routinely ripped off by the Moroccans who are supposed to take care of him. Every now and then an official from the British Embassy in Rabat drops by to see if the old boy is still alive. My English informant, indignant over the way the great man has been treated, asked me, "Now, would the American government let a national hero like Eisenhower or MacArthur live by himself in a shack in Mexico or Guatemala?"

June 2

Memphis Bill Willis calls my house Scorpion Hall, there are so many. I keep viper serum and scorpion serum in the icebox in case someone gets bitten.

With Marguerite McBey, Caroline Duff[1] and M at the annual *moussem* in Tantan. After much haggling we have rented a cavernous goat-hair tent in the nomad encampment outside town. There were camel races, and the festival boomed with the sound of gunfire and drums.

Each day begins with the ritualistic slaughter of a camel. A decrepit, protesting beast is led in from the desert and made to crouch on the sand. A rope is looped around his folded knee to ensure he will never rise again. The head of the animal, whose loud groans indicate he knows his end is near, is forced backwards over the hump, exposing the base of the neck. A black-turbaned bedouin draws from his indigo robe a curved knife which he plunges into the jugular, giving the blade a few twists to widen the hole. The camel emits a swooning groan as the blood gushes out. The head is released, and he is allowed to rest it on the sand for the last few seconds of his life.

Next comes the grisly business of cutting him up. The head is amputated and the hooves lopped off. The belly is split and the guts scooped out. The prized liver is put to one side, and the intestines are emptied and carried away in baskets. The hide is stripped off in one piece. Women gather with buckets to argue over the price of meat. The flies arrive. Soon nothing remains but reddish clots on the sand, lapped by pariahs.

This tent city resembles a fleet of ancient sailing ships moored in confusion. The desert stretches away in every direction, there are miles of empty space all around, but the tents huddle together like a canvas bidonville as though real estate was at a premium. By day they are occupied

---

1. Lady Caroline Duff, a frequent visitor to Tangier.

mainly by women and children, as the men are away tending camels. A maze of ropes webs the spaces between the tents, making passage difficult and sometimes dangerous. Like sailors at sea, women continuously rush out to adjust bucking tent flaps as the wind changes. They pound in stakes and weigh down shifting tent edges with rocks. Violent arguments break out over the ownership of rocks (in a sand desert, rocks are rare), spillage of water and the pranks of wandering children. With the men absent, a libertine, harem-like atmosphere prevails. The temperature is high, few clothes are worn and breasts are casually exposed. The puritanical dress code demanded by the city dwellers is ignored in the Sahara.

The bedouin women who camp outside this oasis are stronger than the village girls. They flaunt a raw elegance that Marguerite terms "how to wear rags." Their physical beauty can be seen through the holes in their blue-black robes as they walk without timidity before men of other tribes. It is a selection of the fittest.

By night the hubbub subsides as the children fall asleep. The flies mercifully depart. Men are about, giving orders. Grown-ups become involved with the all-important business of food and sex. Silhouettes move on the tent walls, and laughter can be heard from within. A flute sounds, a dog barks. The moon shines down on the desert encampment that has gone suddenly still.

July 12, Málaga

Madeleine and I have come here to meet Barley Alison (Alison Press/Secker and Warburg) who is going to publish *Tangier Buzzless Flies* in England.

In the street I ran into Jamie Caffery who was so drunk I don't think he recognized me. This witty, erudite southerner's life is over, drowned in alcohol.

July 14

On the ferry back from Spain I read in the paper that poor Talitha Pol Getty had died of an overdose in Rome. What a beautiful girl. Another lost soul, this one wasted on drugs.

August 10 - Marrakesh

I was standing on Boulevard Mohammed V in Gueliz, waiting for the hardware store to open, when a boy with an orange in his hand dashed from the *marché central*, a berobed merchant in hot pursuit. Without looking right or left, the boy ran headlong into the street. Among the cars parked along the center strip he tripped and fell, both legs sliding beneath the heavy double wheels of a passing bus. I heard the crunching of bones and shrill wail of pain. People were running, but I couldn't look. My face was a reflected mask of anguish among the pots and pans in the window of the hardware store.

September 6

M and I kept vigil by the bed where Ira lay dying. The night was hot, the window was open, and the mournful hooting of an owl in the hospital garden gave us an eerie premonition of what was to come. "They are going to do something awful to me, Johnny," were her last words as they wheeled her off to the operating room. At dawn her kidneys failed. She groaned once and was gone.

In the afternoon I was asked to identify the body for burial. The orderly led me down a flight of stairs to the white, neon-lit hospital morgue pervaded by the sweet and sour smell of unwashed and decaying human flesh. Several cadavers were laid out in a row on a waist-high platform. Sheets were draped over them. The orderly led me to the body on the end, evidently the one that had been most recently added to the row of corpses.

I hesitated; I wasn't sure I could go through with this. A fly was buzzing. Taking a deep breath, I gingerly lifted the corner of the sheet and stared at a female foot. The toes were coloured with bright red polish. Only Ira painted her toenails like that. I let the sheet drop and nodded to the orderly.

October 22 - The Princeton Club of Marrakesh

The Gueliz Post Office is the meeting place for Marrakesh's expatriate community. Over the years I reckon I have established at least a nodding acquaintance with every foreigner who has taken up residence in this Saigon of the Sahara. As mail deliveries outside the city ramparts are unheard of, the oasis dwellers turn up every morning to collect their mail. They come on bicycle or on foot, by donkey or chauffeur-driven limo, depending on their finances or lifestyle. Then they vanish again, without a trace, among the palm trees. What sort of strange, reclusive lives do they lead?

You learn, as soon as you enter the post office, to pick out at a glance your own post box from the bank of hundreds. Your trained and expectant eye instantly detects whether you have mail or not. A light shining through the little window says you're out of luck. The box is empty. A shadow is the tell-tale sign that a treasured letter awaits.

For several days I had noticed that a box near mine was so crammed with mail that not a sliver of light shined through. Had its owner left town, I wondered, dropped dead or cut himself off completely from the outside world?

This morning I came upon a short, bald man tugging the mail from the box. Rather like an overgrown child, he was dressed in a loud striped shirt, white shorts and sandals. Remarkably, his skin was fish-belly white, as though he never ventured out into the broiling Marrakesh sun.

He was sweating with effort. Suddenly his mail cascaded

to the floor. Among the letters I noticed a copy of *The Princeton Alumni Weekly*.

"Did you . . . go to Princeton?" I asked in amazement.

Like a burrowing rodent whose nest you have exposed to the sunlight by lifting a flat rock, the fellow looked up at me with an expression of mingling fear and hatred. Gathering up his mail, he scurried from the post office. I'd never laid eyes on him before and don't expect to again . . .

December 7 - Villa Taylor, Marrakesh

Each day around lunchtime, having worked all morning on *The Flight of the Pelican*, I sit in the car on Boulevard Mohammed V in front of the market making notes of what I will write the next day. As Hemingway said, Quit while you've still got some gas left in the tank. I can't eat, drink, or talk to anyone until I have recorded my ideas. Then I go to market, buy a fish, and take it home and cook it. I rarely write after lunch; my brain goes soft when the belly is full.

Basically, I'm dissatisfied with this book and feel I need to go back to South America to reacquaint myself with the scene.

1972

Yesterday at the Hotel Chems we celebrated the publication of *Tangier Buzzless Flies*. Atheneum cabled a quote from a review by J. R. Frakes in *Book World*: "Albert Camus would have revered this novel."

Linda and Michael Mewshaw[1] turned up with Estelle Parsons who is in Marrakesh filming *Two People*.

After several bottles of champagne we migrated to Tony's Terminal Bar in Marrakesh's industrial quarter.

A French woman screamed from behind a locked door, "You're all a bunch of bastards! To hell with the lot of you!" A wine bottle came flying over the wall, followed by a radio. It shattered on the floor, spilling its guts across the room. The diners were becoming uneasy; they were losing their appetites. Mike demanded an explanation from the patron. Why does he lock up his wife? The Moroccan shrugged: "When she drinks she goes crazy. She breaks things." On this there was general agreement.

May 5

I'd been feeling under the weather for weeks: low, intermittent fever, little appetite or energy. The local French doctor finally prescribed a vermifuge.

I was at Arndt von Bohlen's[2] when a massive urge hit me during lunch. I excused myself from the table and sprinted for the toilet, where I felt something very strange

---

1. American author of *The Toll*; *Year of the Gun*; *Short Circuit* and many other books.
2. Heir to the Krupp fortune who inherited a house in Marrakesh.

come out, followed by a loud splash. Wondering what in the world I'd given birth to, I got down on my hands and knees and peered into the bowl: a knot of six worms, each about five inches long and as thick as my little finger, joined together by what seemed to be a single head.

After that I felt better and ate lunch. Ascari (soldier) worms, they're called.

May 17 - Rabat

The long rides, the wide plains—they never tire me. Space, in the end, always leaves me refreshed.

May 20 - Dakar, Senegal

Joe has been named headmaster of The American School of Tangier. As a member of the Board of Trustees I have come to West Africa to speak at American schools and recruit students.

May 21

Kites and vultures swoop about the hotel . . . toothy heads of weird fish litter the tropical shore, reminding me of La Güera in Sahara Español. Native women parade in stupendous costumes. The gentle voices and distant music, strangely subdued. Long, pointy bowed canoes, laden with rows of black faces, take me back to the Rio Dulce winding through the Guatemalan rain forest. There has been a terrible drought; the upside-down trees have buried their heads in the sand.

May 22

How silver jewelry graces smooth African skin! Today I went to market and bought a Saharan I.D. bracelet to replace the one I lost in Tantan. I wear it on my left wrist. It identifies me with the land where I breathe best.

The sensuality of these African girls. The sheer gaiety of it, the sweetness, the sense of touch that delights. Thus pretty Juliana, whom I met in a High Life dance hall, placed her hand upon my knee and gave it a little squeeze. Laughing, she kissed me on the mouth, a soft sucking kiss from full African lips. She grabbed a piece of my back flesh, and her strong grip spoke of her upbringing as a country girl carrying water from the well. All to reassure me. Yes, the Lebanese boyfriend is a problem. The Lebanese, like all boyfriends, is prone to jealousy and so, rather than make a scene, possibly to ruin an evening which has been so pleasant, so sensuous, with much dancing and drinking from large bottles of green beer, we agreed to meet tomorrow, same dance hall (Star Hotel), 9:30 in the evening.

May 24

"I beg you, sir, I *beg* you give me foreign money."

"You lie, you lie!" (Meaning: you have made a mistake, such as telling the taxi driver to go right instead of left.)

While the brazen, white-throated ravens screeched from the bluff, I helped fishermen pull in their net. Some shrimp, a profusion of shiners, a skate or two. The fishermen stood around (there were about twenty of them) estimating its value.

Juliana's skin (we danced again tonight) is so black that, at times, in the gloom of the club, she seemed to fade from sight altogether. I had before me the vision of her disembodied clothes, wriggling in time to the music, like a puppet on strings, and that Cheshire cat smile—beautiful rows of teeth beneath seductive eyes.

The names of their open-air buses: WISDOM, WASTE NO TIME, GOD NEVER LOSES, WHATEVER YOU DO, FIRM BELIEVER,

May 25 - Lomé, Togo

A grid of red-sand streets, puddled by recent rains, shaded by the ubiquitous *arbre flamboyant*, fronted by a steeply inclined red-sand beach whose main function, judging by the number of turds lying about, is that of the public latrine.

In the public library I have found the senior thesis I wrote at Princeton: *Togoland in Transition*. The pseudo-expert on the country has come to Togo for the first time.

May 26

I was taken to the *marché central*, teeming with Africans selling everything under the sun. I went upstairs to the cloth market, reputed to be the largest in West Africa. The human density was claustrophobic; the heat and smell made my head swim; I stumbled outside to breathe.

May 27 - Lagos, Nigeria

So far this city is living up to its press. As I was having my passport stamped at the airport an argument among police officers quickly degenerated into a bloody brawl with several shots being fired. The road into town was congested by decrepit, wheeled contraptions with angry black faces behind them. The city is so sprawling and trashy (reminding me of Newark, N.J.) that I have yet to get my bearings. Worse, I am confined to a remote embassy apartment *sans* telephone.

The sign in my room:

> MASE TOSI IHIN
> DO NOT URINATE HERE

The prices being ridiculously high and the people being naturally argumentative, I have already become involved in several wrangles with taxi drivers, Hausa traders, *et al.* What is most disconcerting, however, and even a little spooky, making me feel even more dislocated, is that although English has been proclaimed the nation's official language, and despite the fact that most folk speak it, I understand little of what is being said. The shouting match at the airport was conducted in English, yet I could catch only the swear words. I asked a driver to take me to no. 13 Temple Road. He could not understand the number I kept repeating in his ear; he thought I was saying 29. Finally, I wrote it down on a piece of paper. Later we had our own fight, stemming from a misunderstanding over price.

May 28 - Tipping in Lagos:

"Yas, mastah, some dash, mastah."

Something terribly one-dimensional about the tropics: temperature is constant, with little change in season. Same fruit, same foliage, same clothes all year around.

Each day at dusk a tide of fruit bats rises up from the swamps to flap sluggishly through the warm liquid air. Their vast numbers and stilted swarming flight makes me think of pterodactyls.

May 29

A chorus of angry voices woke me in the middle of the night. I went to the balcony and looked down. Along a feebly lit street beneath the palm trees a mob of about twenty people was chasing a man. The man was running, but wasn't sprinting flat out. A tribal matter. Maybe he wanted to be caught and get the punishment over with. As he ran he pleaded over his shoulder and yelped like one already in pain. A high warbling African voice. The mob replied with expressions of bloodthirsty rage.

They caught him on the bridge over a canal. Someone

grabbed his shirt and ripped it. He stumbled, and they fell upon him like a pack of hounds. They beat him, they kicked him, they dragged him around. They cursed him and never stopped punching. He never stopped shrieking— a high, singsong African lament.

In a few minutes it was over. With a few departing kicks they left him, limp and bloody, sprawled on the bridge. Satisfied, the mob broke up and dispersed.

I thought he was dead, but after a few minutes the body on the bridge began to move and moan.

Other things began to move. People started crawling out from under the bridge; they materialized from tall grasses that lined the approaches to the bridge. Each was handicapped in some way. Lurching forward with the aid of crutches or sticks, they warily surveyed the fallen victim. They were joined by legless individuals and other cripples who dragged themselves forward on their hands and knees, or scuttled sideways like crabs.

Like shy but famished jackals they circled the wounded prey. With crutches and sticks they began to beat him, lightly at first, then with a fury. The cries started again. Fortune had brought them someone worse off than they were, and the pariahs and cripples didn't want to miss this opportunity to get in their licks, too.

May 30 - Yaounde, Cameroon

This high jungle town gives off the smells, sights and sounds of Tingo Maria, Peru. The red earth, the chalk-hulled trees, the sound of birds . . . another jungle paradise.

What a relief from the chaos and oppressive atmosphere of Lagos, patrolled by the pistol-packing, machine gun-flaunting military! Yakubu Gowan's entourage whisked past me as I waited for a bus. Twenty or thirty Mercedes filled with round black faces. Armoured cars and trucks with recoilless rifles. Most sinister of all, a Land Rover with a 50 cal. machine gun mounted in back; the teenage gunner, berobed with cartridge belts, swiveling his weapon back and forth, grinning from ear to ear, ready and eager to mow down the adults.

May 31

Proust on Nature: The less she bore man's imprint, the more room she offered for the expansion of his heart.

June 1

A tropical rainstorm burst violently over the town. People scattered like startled sheep, men huddled against walls like rabbits, as the world became a different place. How we hate to get wet! I had just arrived at the café and was able to secure a table beneath an awning. In my shorts, sandals in hand, I have wandered the country roads that lead from village to village. The Africans accost me and ask me to explain my curious habits. It amuses them to see a white man go barefoot.

June 2

When African men shake hands, their palms and fingers touch but do not squeeze; these big strong men, with physiques any artist would pay to draw or sculpt, greet one another with a refined civility and gentleness. They do not presume a show of strength that the firmness of a handshake, as we westerners have been taught to believe, is meant to convey. My grandmother used to say that she could judge a man's character by the strength of his grip and the shine on his shoes.

These men don't even own shoes.

June 3

Elephantiasis is a hideous disease: I looked away from the man's grotesquely swollen leg as I pressed a coin into his hand.

June 22 - Back home in Dar Tounsi

Jean de Breteuil dead of an overdose in Tangier. Twenty-two years old. Poor Boul flew up to identify her "golden boy." Moroccan law dictates that a body may not be moved between April and September because of the heat, so she will have to mourn in private until the end of the summer, when her only son and heir can be buried in the family cemetery in France.

June 29

Kaftan (Ira gave him this name because as a youth he wore colourful robes) hammered on the door of the Petite Maison early this morning. Monsieur Ganya, he said, had not opened the shutters as he always did at 6AM. Through a crack in the shutter Kaftan had seen him "asleep" but could not rouse him. Fearing the worst, I hurriedly dressed and ran through the olive trees to the big house. Peeking through the shutters I made out Ganya's shadowy form in bed. The deathly pallor of his face, framed against the pillows, said all. A sparrow (*tbib*) was perched in his hair. Had its feet become entangled there?

We broke down the door and entered the bedroom. The startled bird darted out the window.

Afterwards Kaftan said he was certain it was Ganya's soul that we saw fly away.

July 3

This is the season when toads, rats and snakes thrive. The oasis seethes with stinging insects, multiplying by the million. My maid, Zahra, has tied a chicken by its foot to her baby's crib. A hungry chicken will eat anything—scorpions, centipedes, tarantulas, even small snakes that could threaten Zahra's new-born babe.

July 4 - Carboneras, Spain

Staying with Barley Alison who has just published *Tangier Buzzless Flies* in London. On my meanderings through these dry, white hills I have come across crumbling irrigation works that date from the time when Andalucia was joined with northern Morocco as an Arab province known as Al-Andalus. When the Moors lived here this part of Spain was a garden; now it is a desert.

July 6 - Málaga

View through a restaurant window (upon looking up from a bowl of *gazpacho*): a Spanish boy was being assaulted by a swarthy gypsy on a park bench. The boy struggled free and ran off; the gypsy picked up his shoeshine box and with a lascivious chuckle wandered toward the next victim.

August 15 - Swaziland

سَفَرْ = safar = trip.

I have come to this corner of Africa chasing a girl who keeps running away from me.

مَاذْلِين = Madeleine.

August 17 - Lourenço Marques, Mozambique, Hotel Cardoso, 1,015 escudos ($50.75), Restaurant Costa del sol (huge shrimp)

Coconut palms lean in the breeze off the Indian Ocean as sailboats race for home. The natives convulse with laughter when one capsizes at the entrance to the harbour. Wide beaches where the tides race and withdraw. At low tide the clam pickers assemble by the water's edge with rakes and baskets. Diminutive human forms are bent in toil over the watery plain.

Land of upside-down trees, cashew and coco groves and the ubiquitous thorn tree. Round gray falcons vie with hornbills and pied crows.

Lateen-rigged dhows cant on the blue horizon; the sight of them fills me with a languid euphoria. Squeaky white sand reminds me of the beach at Gulf Shores, Alabama.

Dhow trip to the Island of Magaruque and return: 600 escudos.

Today M and I travelled through kilometers of dead trees. A disheartening landscape. I would rather be in a rock desert than this wilderness of dying vegetation patrolled by huge white-winged vultures.

Down the alleys of flight . . . these winged predators never fail to fascinate. The ceaseless circling and observation . . . certainly they deserve every scrap they find. The dead and dying, the weak, the young and slow—all belong to them. The snowy-headed, red-lipped, goggle-eyed, broad-winged vulture is a shy creature, for all his awesome equipment.

And so I move through yet another exotic landscape, drawing cosmic and minute conclusions, with my lover whom, in another corner of Africa, I had missed so poignantly. No more can I be lonely, for she is close and tender, admitting that the proximity of these wild animals arouses her sexually.

August 22

One sees the Africans living among the animals—poaching and killing them to be sure—but co-inhabiting this desolate shore in a manner reminiscent of that era when men truly belonged to the animal kingdom. Their grass huts are not much different from the great dark nests eagles make.

August 23 - Gorongoza Game Park

Watery windy plains. "Black Cotton" soil. Hippos roll, cranes fly, the fish eagle keeps watch at the edge of a swamp. The solitary water buck finds partnership with the cattle egret. The rogue elephant flaps his ears and rambles off. Wind brings the smell of rain. The buffalos fix us with a baleful eye. Across the empty space . . . black dots on God's sward . . . a herd of elephants. Shouting angrily at us, a plover protects her nest. Hippos wander freely on the open plain, munching.

Vultures the size of airplanes dry their wings in the treetops after a rain.

Terrorists hide out in the hills: they control about half the country. Any solitary wandering black is a suspect.

August 24 - Salisbury, Rhodesia

This well-laid-out town, immaculate and sterile, represents the white man's determination to impose his idea of order on the African landscape. It speaks of hard work, fear and neglect. What has been neglected is a respect for the dignity of others.

I feel very far from home (Morocco) and homesick.

August 27 - Malkerns, Swaziland

Two native girls, bathing naked in a country stream, beckon and shout to a white man on the dusty road. Black bellies and free, bobbing breasts glisten in the afternoon sun. A few yards across dry elephant grass from the road, they are washing clothes and themselves beneath a stand of sleek, gray-hulled gum trees. When the stranger, after a moment's hesitation, plunges into the grass, the girls shriek, grab for cloth, and run beneath the trees. The older one, however, comes back and brazenly confronts him, puffing out her chest and pressing her fingers into her pendulous breasts, hugely nippled. The younger one stands shyly behind her, clutching smaller breasts with smaller hands. Miriam and Jean. In another minute they are all splashing in the stream. To hell with *bilharzia*.

August 28

The voices of African girls mingle with tremulous laughter. With lightly accented words, clearer than any shouting voice, they do not attempt to overcome distance through lung power. Bright laughter wafts easily on the evening breeze. The breeze likes their language. Lacking harsh consonants, it resembles the calls of the water birds across swampland. Gaiety and laughter hang with woodsmoke on the evening air.

August 29

Recipe for Afrikaans biltong (from Ferdi the cook):

Take strips of meat from the rump of the beast, preferably without sinew, and place them in a bowl (anything but tin) after having sprinkled salt in the bottom. On the first layer sprinkle more salt and pepper and a dash of vinegar. And so on, layer after layer. Allow to stand twelve hours. Turn the whole lot over in the considerable liquid that the salt has drawn from the meat. Let stand another twelve hours. Take the meat out, one strip at a time; with clean hands clean it of muck, dip it in vinegar (to keep off the flies), and hang it on a wire hook.

This should be done in dry weather only. In four days it's ready to eat.

N.B. Garlic may be added to deter flies.

Night fires are burning in the valley and on the hillsides. Night fires are advancing across the African plain like a bloody phalanx. Black silhouettes are leaping among the flames. Small animals take flight, and sleepy birds are airborne. Adios Afrique.

Maholandi (Swazi)—the girl from Holland.

[John Hopkins and Madeleine van Breugel spent the next five months travelling through Central and South America.]

1973

March 18 - Tangier

Upon returning to Morocco after half a year wandering in South America, who is glad to see me? Coco, the parrot.

April 5

The bee eaters (*les chasseurs d'Afrique*), harbingers of spring, have arrived. Chirping whistles fill the air as their Spitfire silhouettes sail on the wind. Coloured green and blue and brown, are these T. Williams' mythological birds that never come down to earth?

May 9 - Jebel Zerhoun near Meknes

These hills that man has touched lightly, not with machines but with his hands, making use of the soil to provide his most basic needs, most soberly testify to his delicate but vital alliance with the earth.

May 12 - Tangier

Jane Bowles dead in Malaga (May 4).

June 5

Today, at a party given by Marguerite McBey for Malcolm Forbes,[1] I met a little girl from Little Rock, Arkansas, Ellen Ann Ragsdale by name, with a perfect peaches-and-cream complexion. And she has read *Tangier Buzzless Flies*. Like my hero Cabell, Ellen Ann has come to Tangier to recover

1. Friend and neighbour of the author's family in New Jersey, who bought the Palais du Mendoub in Tangier.

from the loss of a close friend, Governor Winthrop Rockefeller of Arkansas.

June 8

Tangier City Report: Weather balmy. People stroll the boulevard looking brown from the beach, clean from the sea, free in their light summer clothes. A naval ship is in port, and young, bearded, tattooed sailors are making the shopkeepers happy.

July 23

Last night I threw a Jilala party on the terrace of the Gazebo for Tennessee, who apologetically returned a wrinkled, water-warped copy of *Tangier Buzzless Flies*. The book had fallen into the bath tub at the Minzah Hotel.

After the party, Tennessee: "You're sweating, boy, you've worked yourself into a lather. Now go shower down and come back and dance some more!"

July 26

Bobo Legendre[1] is back in town. Morocco speaks to her in a way no other place does. At the party she claimed to have levitated and circled the olive tree three times while still in a sitting position. I say the Jilala beat did the lifting.

July 28

There have been many magic moments for Ellen Ann and me this summer: swimming off the rocks at Jew's River at dawn; climbing the Old Mountain at midnight while the lighthouses of Tarifa and Malabata flash together, their signals proclaiming the momentary placidity of the untethered sea. Picking up the Jilala musicians in the street:

1. American journalist and painter.

142

they were on their way from one wedding to another, walking to save carfare, and they played their *bendirs* and *shebabas* in the back seat of my car as we cruised the dark streets toward yet another fiesta. And myself alone—running, walking, searching for the missing shell, prostrate upon the sand, leaping into cool waves for liquid refreshment, gloriously alone upon the North African strand.

August 5 - 35 today

This morning Ellen Ann and I walked onto the terrace at dawn. Below us a cat was returning from a night of hunting in the garden. An owl flew soundlessly through the trees. The grace of its flight, the stealth of the cat's step, the deep shadows in the garden where pockets of night still lingered, and above all the astonishing quantity of light that was pouring across the watery horizon from the Pillars of Hercules. It all seemed so wild, so silent and mysterious that we didn't dare move. We could have watched it forever because we loved being part of it.

August 7

Madame Perla (the Spanish fortune teller): her cards say that I stand on the threshold of a mystery that will influence the rest of my life.

September 5 - Walking along the Atlantic beach from Cape Spartel to Asilah.

At 7:30 I helped three young fishermen slide their boat into the sea. At noon I came upon a black fin whale—dead.

September 7 - Tangier

These shining days—I never get enough of them. As a prelude to autumn, cloud formations have broken up and departed. Summer haze has dissolved before a freshness of air, and new vistas are being opened on every hand.

Spain is clear, as is Gibraltar, as are all the sea lanes between the Atlantic and the Mediterranean.

September 10 - The Sahara:
Leonum Arida Nutrix—Arid Nurse of Lions (Horace)

The streets of Marrakesh are nearly deserted. The earth has given up all resistance to the heat, and the wind blowing in from the desert sucks up whatever moisture remains in the soil. Walls of airborne sand obscure the sun but do not diminish its power. Swirls of dust coast along the Djemaa el Fna carrying a newspaper gone berserk in the wind. Heat occupies the town as the Moroccans hide behind the thick walls of their mud houses.

When the sun goes down, the people of Marrakesh, dressed in light cotton robes, glide along speaking in whispers. This is the hour of the evening prayer. During the summer, the cafés of Marrakesh are moved from street level to rooftop to take advantage of the breezes. Rugs are spread on terraces, and customers gather beneath the stars to drink mint tea and talk, all the while gazing over the cubist rooftops of their desert city. The minarets point toward eternity. If this architectural message goes unheeded, the muezzin's echoing calls inject into the time-absolving conversations of the café dwellers harmonic reminders of their duty toward God.

September 18 - Dar Tounsi

Walloped two scorpions today—bad ones. Found them in the cellar among a mass of black beetles beneath a discarded birdcage. An ugly scratching noise, so loud I thought it was a rat. A sinister assemblage.

November 5

This novel, *The Flight of the Pelican*, is giving me fits! To get away from it I have typed up my South American diaries.

It's another book.

December 20

High winds arrived yesterday and blew all night with a force that frightened us. The wind tore out of the west, the direction from which all rains must come. One cypress, which grows beside the well, thrashed violently but did not fall. The other grows on the southeast corner. I also feared for the eucalyptus which are highly vulnerable to windstorms, but they survived with the loss of one fallen branch. Madeleine hopes the whole grove will fall down. I also feared for the water reservoir which perches above us on the roof. These are the fears the wind brings. Today the skies took on many strange colours. It was a violent, wrenching morning. Sunlight glittered off the snow fields on the High Atlas; later the wind dropped, the clouds clotted together, and the rain began to fall. The wind continues to moan about the mud corners and date palms, and the rain has not stopped.

We live close to nature in the oasis—nature that is breathtaking in its beauty and sometimes frightening in its violence. Huddled in front of the fireplace, we feel secure in this mud house, but not invulnerable.

December 26

Yesterday M and I went to the Ait Ouirir market in search of a Christmas donkey, a small one to replace Tirbosh, who died of tetanus. Due to heavy rains and the high prices enforced by the government, few countrymen had come to market. We tramped through the mud and bought 7 3/4 litres of fresh olive oil. Even the price demanded for this basic commodity seemed excessive: 6DH/litre.

At noon we drove up the Ourika valley. Heavy rain in the valley had been accompanied by deep snowfalls in the Atlas. The scene before us, as we approached those cloud-shrouded peaks, was like a black-and-white photo. Gray clouds clotted the black ridges and the snow fields; no other colour to be seen.

1974

January 9 - Marrakesh

Sitting in the sun having a coffee by the *marché central*, I noticed that the fellow next to me had begun to scratch. He clawed at himself like a madman, or one who has been overrun by a legion of fleas. First it was his hands he flailed against each other; then the wrists he rubbed together with the tenacity of a boy scout with two sticks. Then his ankles, knees, thighs, ribs and back. The chair and table were rocking. When I got to my feet to leave, he snatched my coffee glass and drained the dregs. "*Merci*," he murmured, smiling sheepishly.

January 25 Dar Tounsi

The French writer Gabriel Matzneff visited me at the Petite Maison. An amiable, balding, monklike figure, he helped me chop wood and carry logs to make a fire. We pumped water from the well and fed the donkey. We lit the kerosene lamps and hung them on the walls. After a few drinks we drove to Marrakesh and dined on stuffed camel's intestines at one of the innumerable makeshift restaurants that Moroccans set up each night on the Djemaa el Fna.

Today I read a newspaper article he wrote about the visit, in which he expressed his disappointment at finding my way of life too civilized.

February 3

Today is the Ashoura. The children have been given drums

and are making music. Last night, great bonfires were lit in the palmeraie and in town. Bands of children dance by leaping flames. Their growing numbers convince them that the streets belong to them. They may be right about this.

February 5

Abdelkader, the "crazy one", spends his days and nights by the roadside. He will not take money from passers-by, but bread is accepted with a dazzling smile.

February 6

ZZ, a witch, practices black magic. To some her eyes say, "Come here!" to others, "Go away!"

February 8

Hasnaoui, the disgruntled Moroccan intellectual. Also my Arabic teacher.

"Another mosque!" He laughs sardonically. "Just what we need."

"Have you ever seen a more idiotic sight in your life than a veiled woman driving an automobile?" (The driving school is located next door to his bookshop.)

"Moroccan female dress—it may look exotic to a foreigner, but the sooner our women adopt western clothes, the better. All those layers of djellabas and pantaloons prevent them from washing. Our women are dirty."

He looks disgusted, fed up with the backwardness of people.

"Arabic? Don't bother to learn it. It's useless in the modern world. In fifty years it'll be as dead as Latin."

He likes to go to bars and spends Ramadan in Spain.

"English is the language. English, English, English. Forget the others."

February 28 - مُراكش

The old potter was pleased with his work. As he dusted off each plate and handed them to me one by one, a serenely proud smile wreathed his face. Those wise old hands had sculpted them from mud. With affection approaching love the potter ran his fingers over his works of art. He pointed to his signature on the back and the magic stone that had smoothed them. Following his instructions, I have dipped each in water and, when they were dry, gave each a light coating of olive oil. The water and oil were quickly absorbed. According to the potter and his son, the plates will "drink less now."

The potter's grandson, aged five, placed a hand upon my shoulder (I was seated on the floor) and lectured me on the virtues of bread, oil, light bulbs, bicycle chains and the other essentials of life.

March 1

A letter from the desert: my guides are waiting in M'hamid to lead me into the Sahara. I'm looking forward to the adventure, but wish I had someone to share it with. But as Norman says in *All I Wanted Was Company*: "Sometimes one doesn't have any choice in the matter."

March 4 - *Chez Zézé, Marrakesh.*

Ellen Ann has gone back to Little Rock. I am here, reading a review of *Les Mouches de Tanger* (just published in Paris by Gallimard) in the Moroccan newspaper *Le Maghreb*, entitled: QUELLE MOUCHE A PIQUÉ JOHN HOPKINS?

March 5

What was recently a lush green field is now cracked and dry. The hungry animals have devoured even the stubble. The storks who hunted frogs have departed, taking the frogs with them. The caterpillars have become moths and have flown away. Only the black beetles remain. And me. Scorpions and vipers inhabit the surrounding rocks.

March 6

This afternoon I attended Rom Landau's[1] funeral at the International Cemetery. Afterwards I stood for a few minutes by Ira's and Ganya's graves. They are now adorned with Russian Orthodox crosses, courtesy of their friend Robert Gerofi.[2] Then off to the market to make final purchases for the desert trip.

March 8

The history of colonial Marrakesh is recorded in the tombstones of the International Cemetery.

Tomorrow I depart.

March 9 - Ouarzazate

The desert is quiet. The evening sky swarms with migrating kites. When I step onto the balcony and with deep breaths inhale the solemnity of the Sahara, a peace enters me. This soothes me temporarily.

I envy the kites' flight, their wildness, their freedom, their apparent unconcern. And the desert is clean.

I stand before the desert. I cannot say I look forward to crossing it. The desert dogs are barking, and the wind is rising. The night wind that moans under the door seems to bear a special message for me.

March 10 - Zagora

I'm a bit more elevated tonight. I've been to the top of a

1. Author of *Morocco; God is My Adventure; Minos the Incorruptible; Paderewski; Pilsudski, Hero of Poland,* and other books.
2. Belgian architect residing in Tangier. In 1993 he was awarded *l'Ordre de Mérit* for services to the French nation.

mountain to view the desert at sunset. The vast stony silence makes me think of the judgement of God. The Sahara cannot be home for any outsider except for someone who passionately wishes it to be so.

March 11 - M'hamid Al Ghazlane

The deal has been made. 500 DH.[1] A white *fokia*, or light cotton robe, is also being made. The camels have been brought in from the desert, or will be in the morning. Tomorrow we will set off. Three men, three camels. Seven days. I'm feeling adventurous.

The guide, Loot, has returned to his tent. The local *practicante* has been generous: Vit C, anti-dysentery pills, anti-scorpion and anti-viper serum. I have the syringes.

Tomorrow, I shall find out about camels, but tonight a Berber group from Khemisset is in town—with tattooed dancing girls!

March 12

As soon as I put on these Saharan clothes I feel comfortable.

2:30PM. We finally set off at noon. After walking and riding, we have stopped for tea. This is the Draa Valley. Sand dunes and scrub. Amidst so much desolation, a little bird makes a whistle like a man might make. It flew up and down, whistling; kind of spooky, it seemed to be beckoning me toward the void.

2:46. The camels are hobbled and the sheep is tethered to a bush. Loot gathers twigs and makes tea.

2:55. A hole is scooped from the dune to protect the fire from the wind. A single match lights twigs as dry as tinder.

3:28. A man approaches. A single human voice raised

1. About $100.00.

in song fills an entire desert.

5:00. We have stopped to pitch camp. I figure we've made 15 km. (4km./hour). Two others have joined us. Camels graze around us in the desert, including one snow-white mother and baby. People are about. Loot prays; a knife is being sharpened; the sheep's end is near.

6:12. The voices of the Saharans are uniform; they are gentle but can be raised and carry a long way. These must be the ancient voices of people who have not gathered in sufficient numbers or lack sufficient reason to form permanent communities.

I spy a jet stream, heading north toward Paris while I plod south toward nothingness. Tonight the passengers will dine on the boulevard, while I . . . (the sheep's throat has just been cut).

Camels respond to the gentlest tug. (The rein is a string attached to the beast's left nostril.) I find them compatible, the pace easy and the sway not uncomfortable. They know where they're going. They know the best paths (the sandy ones). Good companions.

Like the writing of a novel, progress across the desert is ineluctably slow. The only way to get anywhere is to keep at it day after day after day.

The desert. Is this what I've wanted?

I've got it whether I want it or not.

Sun going down; wind going down.

Brahim makes sand bread. We eat the inner organs of the sheep, talk about desert crossings, and drink glass after glass of tea. I'm so tired I could sleep on a bed of nails.

March 13 - الصبح

Started off at 8.

Gazelle tracks.

Fossils everywhere.

Stones that glitter like crystal and ring together like steel.

At 11:30 we stopped in a sandy river bottom for lunch consisting of last night's bread, cheese and an orange. My ass is sore, my legs and feet are sore as hell.

Loot: full of energy and cheer. Now he makes tea again. Forty-two years old, only seven more than I, he looks fifty-five. He's been to Taodeni twice, long ago, when the French ruled the desert.

1:33. Ugh! It's hot and there's no shelter from the sun. Flies are relentless. Days like this I wish I were back in New Jersey.

Now a cool breeze arrives and makes all the difference.

These people waste more water than the Mauritanians, who never wasted any, as far as I could see. Here tea glasses are washed with water, not scoured with sand. Then, there is more water here, and our trip is not long.

In the Sahara, one must be impeccable, never fastidious.

5:37. We are now encamped in the river bed. Big dunes all around; tomorrow we will see nothing but sand.

I figure we made 28 km. today.

Loot says 30.

Brahim says 35.

We are about 5 km. from Sidi Abdelrahman, 45 km. from M'hamid.

Brahim says we made 3 km./hour.

I figure 4.

We now number 7 men, 4 camels, 4 asses.

At Sidi Abdelrahman, a small, primitive oasis and holy shrine where we stopped this afternoon to wash and drink, folded *haimas* (tents) and other desert equipment wrapped in neat bundles were perched on rocks and in the branches of the trees. The Saharans sometimes deposit this heavy baggage for years at a time, where it is never molested because the Saint guards it. A strange, spooky place, with birds. Frogs croaked lugubriously in the spring. I'm glad we didn't spend the night there.

It's been a long day. Up at dawn, and we didn't pitch camp until 6.15PM. Sore but feeling well. A thoroughly desolate, uninteresting landscape. A sloping, pebbly plain between the jebel and the oued. Both miles distant in the shimmering heat. Boring. Tiring. Dull. Tough going. My feet are killing me.

I look forward to the sand.

I've smoked my last cigarette.

My body burns from the sun and the hard going, but I feel OK.

My djellaba, burnoose, silver bracelet, Swiss knife, especially my writing fascinate all.

Loot is the old desert hand, but Brahim seems to know the route as well as he does.

Loot says the trip to Taodeni took 37 days not pressing the pace. Another 28 to Timbuktoo, making 65.

7:39PM. These desert people talk and talk. All they do is talk—in long monologues, to be answered by another, longer monologue. To get away from it, to enjoy the silence of my mood, I walk behind the camels and search for fossils.

Their way of eating, which I find sensible, is to eat something right away when a stop is made, even if it is only a crust of yesterday's bread. This cuts the appetite, and one waits patiently while the hot meal is prepared. To be in a hurry in the desert can be fatal. You leave things behind; you take the wrong path.

When they pray it is briefly and casually. Less affected by the formalities of Islam than city people, with little or no opportunity to visit a mosque, desert folk live their whole lives out of doors, beneath this "sheltering sky." The sky is their religion; it forms the prism through which man and God behold each other.

Brahim is making sand bread. An arduous procedure, but the result is excellent.

He reminds me of Driss Drissi because he can be both playful and authoritative. Also because of his narrow shoulders. Also his voice. Also because he comes from an influential family.

Loot holds the young fellows with his tales. He knows my age and I know his. We smile at each other. From our faces, it is clear that my life has been easy, soft and protected; he has spent the whole of his exposed to the elements. Elements will take their toll.

The drive into the desert:

When I arrived in ugly Ouarzazate, my cozy mud house in the palmeraie of Marrakesh that I had just left seemed like paradise.

When I got to Zagora, even dullsville Ouarzazate seemed like paradise.

When I got to treeless M'hamid, the beautiful Zagora oasis seemed like paradise.

Here in this tent, now even a one-horse town like M'hamid seems like paradise.

The paradise I yearn for may well be right here in this miserable tent.

I lie on a rug before a candle stuck in the sand. Outside, a few feet away, a fire blazes, men talk, a pot bubbles and the stars shine down on a perfectly still Saharan night.

Last night we ate the sheep's intestines and internal organs; tonight it's the head and shins. Even the bones are cracked between the teeth and sucked clean of marrow. "Praise be to God" is what Loot says every time he (or anyone else) burps.

A shooting star. I make the usual wish.

One of our companions is a slave. Black and subdued, he receives the poorest share of food and performs the heaviest tasks. Nevertheless he has a big smile and laughs hilariously at the silliest jokes. He eats and lives with us, but takes orders and in general is treated as an inferior. He evidently knows his place and so, apparently, does everyone else. A gentle form of servitude.

Sand bread. Scooping a hole in the sand, Brahim kindled a fire of sticks. When the fire was reduced to a mound of glowing embers, he scraped the embers to the perimeter of the basin and flopped the round flat dough onto the hot sand. (NB: hot sand flows like mercury.) The dough, made of flour, a pinch of yeast, salt and water, had already been kneaded and allowed to stand for a while in a bucket. With the dough resting where the fire had been, Brahim covered it with a layer of hot sand.

While we waited, Loot prayed. His prayer in no way resembles the orthodox, humble mutterings of men lined up in mosques. He didn't go down on his knees. He just stood atop a sand dune and shouted at God. The high trailing voice was suspended in the silence of the evening sky. His chanting seemed to fill the empty space for miles around.

After about three-quarters of an hour, Brahim majestically lifted a large white loaf from the dune. Incredibly, not one grain of sand was stuck to it. Then, for reasons I did not fully understand, he rather unceremoniously beat it with a stick before reburying it in cold sand for a few minutes.

When the meat was cooked, Brahim ripped the bread apart, releasing a cloud of steam, and we dipped the pieces in the stew. The meat was placed to one side to await the "desert lottery."

Can't stop thinking about Sidi Abdelrahman, with its primitive Koubba and cemetery. I'm glad we got out of there; even the palm trees looked sick. And I refuse to drink that water, even if it's boiled. I keep thinking of Vieuchange.

Saharans talk about money all the time. They haggle for hours over pennies. This is the margin they live on.

One consumes, on the average, a dozen small glasses of the strong smoky sweet green tea per day. No mint. Most liquid is taken in this manner.

March 14

After getting a late start (9AM) because the camels had strayed, we stopped early (10.30) for lunch, on the edge of the great dune desert. Once we enter here, there will be nothing for the camels to eat for a day or two, so we shared an early lunch while they grazed on the bushes they love so much.

The gait of a camel: although she appears to move both legs on one side forward at the same time, this is not exactly so. The smaller hind leg moves first, practically kicking the forefoot from its place. So while the foreleg moves forward, the hind foot is already planted, providing greater solidity.

Our companions have gone off to their tents. Loot, Brahim and I are alone. Better this way.

I figure we drink 12 glasses of tea per day:

     3 breakfast
     3 lunch
     3 evening stop
     <u>3</u> dinner
     12

Beni (Oulad) Sibi, here.

Loot has never been to Marrakesh or Ouarzazate, but he knows the Sahara as far as Taodeni.

It has been more or less agreed that we have made about 20 km. although Loot maintains we are now some 80 km.

from M'hamid. Don't know how we could be that far.

I'm exhausted, the feet are sore, and the toes have blood blisters. Even the camels are bushed. One collapsed this afternoon. "Dog!" Loot snarled, as he yanked it to its feet. No place for the weak in the desert. For most of the afternoon we wandered through the dunes, which are beautiful to look at but make for rough going—up and down, through deep sand. I started off barefoot, but the sand scorched the soles of my feet, which accounts for the soreness. Even in sandals it was too hot to walk, so I mounted my camel.

The pace was slow, as we allowed the camels to browse on green shrubs. It was hot and tiring among the dunes and, as beautiful as they are, I was glad to be out of them.

Then we crossed a dreary plain littered with dead bushes. I was depressed and wished to be anywhere but on a camel heading into a violent landscape. My life seems wrong; I'm not making anybody happy. I need a wife. My writing, like this camel trip, is a voyage into nothingness. Camels to nowhere.

We are now encamped near the River Draa. I say river but there is no water. Firewood has been collected, the tent pitched, and we're on our third cup of tea.

Two boys appeared, one with the looks of the young Albert Camus. They were only ten or so but possessed the gravity of adults and were treated as men. Their father was killed in the fighting at Hassi Beida.

Now that I think about it, it's amazing how Algerian Camus looked. Not *pied noir* but tense, intellectual, Berber—one of the FLN that fought the French army to a standstill in 1962.

Brahim (Boahanin) and I have been discussing his brother's death. *Mektoub*. Killed on the road between Ouarzazate and Adgz (Beni Saoun), buried in Ouarzazate. Twenty-four years old.

Seven o'clock: sun going down. It's warm and windless. Fire burning. I've eaten two boiled eggs. Feeling better, as depression departs along with fatigue, boredom and hunger. I must experience this trip in retrospect before casting dreary judgements upon my life.

These desert people have nothing. Their land produces nothing. They're probably the poorest people in the world. They are able to live on less than most people, but the fact remains that they are very poor.

Loot has two camels, nothing else.

Brahim claims he feels weak in M'hamid. The same in Marrakesh. To feel strong he must go into the desert.

Loot (Miloud) ben Mohamed ben Tayyet ben Hussein ben Musa.

Brahim ben Abdelrahman ben Bashi ben Buari ben Faragi.

Loot has teeth trouble. He chews tobacco mixed with ashes from the fire. This, he says, dulls the pain.

These people live with physical pain all their lives, while we are anguished by the mental. Their pain is assuaged by perfect spiritual assurance, while ours is aggravated by doubt. All their lives they have slept beneath the stars, where the spirit expands to fill the empty space, while our souls suffer from "cabin fever".

Brahim's beautiful voice dispels loneliness.

I say 22 km.

Loot says 30 km.

B   "   20 "

We are now encamped with another caravan, belonging to the son of one of the largest camel owners in the Draa Valley. Eight hundred camels. I told him I'll buy camels from him when I travel to Taodeni. He covets my Swiss knife.

I have played doctor, opening and daubing with disinfectant cream two nasty infections.

Also with the group is a Marabout, or holy man. He suffers from stomach and chest pains which I guess to be caused by liver, for which I have no cure. He has just led our group in desert prayer. Brahim has prayed for the first time. He's now making bread.

One man has a certificate he is proud of. It allows him to pass where others are stopped. It is issued by the Gendarmerie Royale in Ksar-es-Souk and says he deserted from the French army in 1961, armed with a pistol, 39 rounds of ammo, and six grenades.

This morning, just after setting out, we came across a member of the Camel Corps, which patrols this part of the Moroccan desert. Sitting high on a camel, armed with a rifle, dressed ordinarily, that is in a blue robe crisscrossed with white sashes, his skin jet black, the features fine Arab. Handsome and haughty, he did not greet me, but glanced suspiciously in my direction as he exchanged salaams with the others. He looked cruel and beautiful and hard as nails. Let's face it, the King of Morocco has some toughies on his side.

We rode for a couple of hours before joining another group of Saharans with about forty camels. These belong to the father of the son with whom we are now encamped. We were not allowed to approach because women were present. We saw their camels with wide canopied saddles designed for them and their babies.

We lunched in the dunes. It was too hot with no cover. The exposed meat drew a cloud of flies. I was thoroughly uncomfortable while waiting for B and Loot to fetch water from a well (Hassi). Ali, 10, entertained me with songs from Mauritania and showed me his Spanish knife. In a wasteland like this a Spanish knife has the entertainment value of the Marx Bros.

For four hours we marched across dunes and rocks to arrive once more on the banks of the Draa.

The Marabout's name: Sidi Azzouz ben Sidi Larbi ben Sidi Hamid ben Sidi Mahdani ben Sidi al Hadj ben Sidi Brahim ben Sidi Shiek.

Son of camel owner (infection on foot): Si Hamadi ben Sidi el Hadj ben Ali ben Abdullah ben Bomadama. Friend with infection on nose: Si Bashir ben Bon Bakal ben Moktar ben Hamid ben Naji ben Mohamed.

The others: Moulay ben Boujma ben Ali ben bel Hadj ben Hamdi.

Mohamed ben Hamou ben Moha ben Hussein.

They like to watch me write their names down. As they are illiterate, writing has an almost magical connotation for them.

March 16

The road to Taodeni, according to Loot:

From M'hamid to Hammada 3 days

Hammada	6	"
Sand	7	"
Mountains	8	"
Sand	6	"
Hammada	5	"
Mixed	4	"

This does not include days of rest, stops to feed the camels and to replenish supplies at wells and water holes.

This was not via Tindouf, which would take longer.

One would take: dry vegetables, onions, carrots, etc. They know how to dry them in M'hamid. Also dry meat. Biltong. (See Swazi recipe.) A carbine to shoot gazelle on the Hammada. Rice, chick peas, dry peas, couscous, flour, etc. Pasta. Dry things.

We sat beneath a tree in the middle of this plain that clipped the horizon in every direction and discussed the problems of travelling to Timbuktoo. As we haven't far to go today it's been decided to prolong this pleasant interlude by preparing more tea.

Brahim is as playful as a puppy. He kids Loot, who can think only of his stomach. He ate too much last night. Our host's bread did not agree with him.

Loot: a big strong camel can carry 160 kilos, or 160 litres of water. We will need three camels, carrying approx. 500 litres of water, three camels for food, and one for the tent and medicine. Seven baggage camels in all. Riding camels take the rider only, plus a few personal items— binoculars, camera, rifle.

One essential item for any lengthy Saharan journey, it dawned upon me this afternoon at the well where we watered the camels, would be a length of rope and a bucket for drawing water. Many Saharan wells are filled with sand, and these items would be required for clearing the well. (One man would have to descend.)

I say 23 km. today.

Wells to Taodeni: they vary from every third day to every sixth day.

Loot is skeptical.

He won't let me make bread because he's sure it'll make him sick.

He thinks the desert trip might be too tough for me.

He'd come, however, if I hired an experienced guide (better two guides).

9:34PM. When I walk away from camp at night to be alone, I take in the stars. They flash and twinkle and seem to move. (When I see a shooting star, I always make the same wish.) The stars seem to buzz and sing, as if each were giving off a minute remote vibration which I alone am picking up. The world is silent, the desert and darkness around me are silent, unless there's a wind, but the stars are definitely not silent. They're ringing!

But when the wind begins to rise in the middle of the night, when unknown things begin to move about, and the world beneath the moon seems a ghastly place, one is thankful for one's companions, the camel-men, their peaceful sleeping forms a few feet away.

In a week from now I'll miss this desert and stars and peace of mind. I shall be looking back upon these lonely nights with love and longing.

March 17 - الصبح ده

Their women are treated as separate entities, a race apart, foreigners to men's ways as we are to theirs. We've just had couscous in Loot's *haima*, prepared by Loot's women who occupy the same tent, but are separated by a cloth partition and are unseen by us.

Loot's wife is about thirty. Married at twelve, she has produced six children. Looks fifty, but it's a cheering sight when that leathery face breaks into laughter. Negro blood in both her and Loot.

The ritual of these people's lives is based on the fulfilment of elemental requirements, dramatically underscored by the scarcity of all goods.

1. The distance to the well and the quality of the water in it.
2. Spinning goat hair into thread.
3. The ritual of making bread.
4.   "   "   "   "   tea.

Men and women join together, mate together and stay together for the sake of survival. Children are the binders; that's where the love goes.

My candles are greeted as a luxurious indulgence.

March 18

Much fresher, and a diversion from heavy human considerations, were the tiny tracks I discovered at dawn. An entire night's theatre had left its traces on the sand. If there has been no wind, I can easily follow the progress of the actors.

A mouse highway connected two clumps of bushes atop separate dunes. A vulture or eagle (*hibara*) had landed and stalked from one mouse castle to another, seeking stragglers or the unwary. The scorpions had gone on parade, and a serpent had glided from one bush to the next, leaving a sinister track of a stealthy mission. The beetles had held a dance or a war, and lizards had raced by.

I followed the drama where the eagle had trapped a mouse, and where the snake throttled a lizard, and where a lizard swallowed its favourite insect. A scuffle among bugs had temporarily rumpled the palimpsest of sand. Soon the wind will erase these marks, clearing the stage for another evening's entertainment.

The beetle's trail is haphazard and weary. I have seen it toil uphill, like Sisyphus, fighting a miniature cascade of sand created by its own efforts.

Yesterday we saw a gazelle; there were tracks where a swift shy one wandered from one bush to another, grazing. The tracks of a stalking jackal followed. His trail was straightforward and purposeful as he followed the scent. He was catching up.

Also for the desert:

Wooden bowl for couscous	Poncho
Special boxes for tea, etc.	Taifor
Rifle	Biltong
Binocs	Mortar and pestle
Funnel	Sewing kit
Cooking pot with top, tripod etc.	
String for tying things on	

Today: 14 km.

Damas is commonly played with camel turds and pieces of straw, on a board drawn in the sand which looks like this:

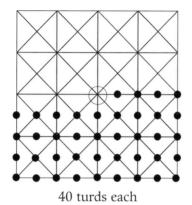

40 turds each

March 19

Their ability to see far exceeds my own. They know a man is walking toward us before I see him. They have been observing his progress while I am unaware of his presence. They know what to look for. They know the significance of all distant heat-distorted movements. They know where men live, and from which direction to expect them. They know what camels like to eat; they expect to see them browsing on certain kinds of shrubbery. Where there are camels there will be men.

March 20

This morning I looked down at my feet. I can't remember what they were like before, but now they look different. More like hooves than feet. If I ever put on shoes again, I'll have to buy new shoes.

The Hammada is littered with fossils. Water animals

trapped in stones. The world has become unrecognizable.

March 25 - مُراكش

The trip back from the desert.

When I returned to M'hamid, the tent I had left behind seemed like paradise;

When I checked into the luxury hotel in Zagora, a primitive place like M'hamid seemed like paradise;

When I got to Ouarzazate, Zagora seemed like paradise;

Back here in my cozy house outside Marrakesh, now even a dump like Ouarzazate seems like paradise.

This is what the desert does. It leaves you with a terrible nostalgia for the purity you left behind. That purity was you. The intense discomfort of desert travel sharpens the experience and makes the memory more poignant.

March 27

My friend Abdelkader, the road hermit.

This morning he was covered in blood. Was he hit by a car? Attacked by dogs? Deaf and dumb, he cannot tell me. He only smiles and accepts my donation of bread and Bandaids.

March 29

I'm trying to decipher what I scribbled on the margins of *Le Matin* chez Mme. Zézé, where I needed several beers to cool off from a hangover. Across the street my car was being hammered back into shape (unbearable racket). It all started when Bill Willis invited me to dinner to meet David[1] and Jocelyn Dimbleby. Having just returned from the desert, I hadn't had a drink in two weeks. Expecting to find Madeleine at Dar Tounsi, I came back to an empty

1. B.B.C. television presenter.

house. Not even a letter. Solitude in the desert is one thing; loneliness in my own home is another.

To make matters worse spring has roared into Marrakesh. Wind and rain one minute, sun the next. Temperamental weather always makes me nervous. After several maddening calls on the oasis telephone, I got hold of her mother in Holland who told me she was still in Milan with her friends. I felt I'd been slapped in the face.

As a consequence of all this I had too much to drink at Bill's. Way too much. On the way home I drove straight into a mud wall at Bab el Khemis. I couldn't believe my bleary eyes: I'd missed the arch by about four feet! How I made it home I'll never know. I remember a terrible grinding noise. The next day the car had to be towed to Marrakesh and the fender pried off the wheel. The only thing I remember about the party is Jocelyn Dimbleby volunteering to find me a wife. An English wife. It sounds almost exotic.

April 2

On the Royal Air Maroc flight from Marrakesh to Italy (chasing Madeleine):

I was sitting next to Anthony Quinn who has been in Marrakesh filming the life of Mohammed the Prophet. The plane stopped in Casablanca where Hamri the painter, portfolio under his arm, leaped aboard. He was going to have a show in Italy. Hamri gets turned on by famous people. When he spotted me with Quinn he started jumping around like a Mexican jumping bean. Jabbering in Spanish, brandishing his pictures, he finally ended up in Quinn's lap. Quinn loved it and finally caved in. He bought a painting for cash. Hamri winked at me. He was stony broke. Now he can pay for his hotel in Rome.

May 6 - Back at Dar Tounsi

A sparrow sits on the branch of an olive tree, fluttering in sexual anticipation. Her mate alights beside her, shoves a huge worm down her throat and flies off. She looks about, worm hanging from her beak, completely nonplussed.

May 16 - Haut Atlas

The past four days I have spent climbing Jebel Toubkal, Morocco's highest peak. All afternoon I trudged through deep snow up a long narrow valley. The river, as it sluiced along the ravine below me, had thrown up fantastic ice configurations. Icicles as thick as a man's waist clung to the cliffs where water trickled in the sun. The snowfields reflected a light that was almost blinding. I was smart to have brought my dark glasses along. Hardly a breath of air stirred. Snow plumes trailing from peaks far above me indicated, however, that strong winds were blowing at higher altitudes. I was glad I wasn't up there. When long blue shadows began to flow down from the ridges, I kept an anxious eye out for the refuge.

A ray of sun glinted off a tin roof up ahead. The Berber who came out to greet me wasn't dressed in a djellaba. He was wearing instead knickerbockers and mountain boots, a quilted parka, wool cap and goggles—all in a used condition.

When I awoke the next morning the sun was shining. Downstairs I found Miloud brewing a pot of tea. He greeted me in his usual hearty manner and asked if I were ready to tackle the mountain. He pointed out the window at a great blue wall leading up to a gap between two towering cliffs. Following his instructions, I stuffed the cuffs of my trousers into my socks and wrapped strips of cloth around my legs from ankle to knee, in the form of puttees.

After a breakfast of bread and butter and several glasses

of tea, Miloud handed me a pair of gloves and some ear-muffs, and we set off. Crossing the river on a snow bridge, we attacked the mountain. It wasn't straight up, as it had appeared from the refuge, but the slope was so steep that I felt like a fly. Kicking footholds into the frozen snow, Miloud led the way. I followed on all fours, like a monkey or a bear. We hadn't climbed for more than five minutes before I had to sit down and rest. Collapse might be a better word—my lungs were bursting.

In an hour we passed from beneath the cliffs into a wide white basin, where we had a view of the crest with its trailing plume of snow. Miloud began to whoop and hol-ler, and I feared his booming peals would loosen the drifts above us. On the contrary, the voice of one small man dominated the solemn peaks all around. It was inspiring to hear him bellow like that, so I yelled along with him at the top of my lungs. Together we startled a crowd of croak-ing ravens, and the impassive mountains returned our voices. It was as though we two were the only men alive, and the world was beginning, or had recently come to an end.

We mounted the high basin wall, where Miloud pre-sented me with an incomparable view from the edge of the mountain. The precipice fell away a thousand feet or more; even the eagles swirled far below us. South from the chain of the Atlas, which resembled giant scoops of vanilla ice cream, Miloud pointed out the Jebel Sarhro beyond Ouarzazate, the valleys carved by the rivers Dra and Souss, and the Anti Atlas, which forms the final bar-rier to the desert. We could even make out the edge of the Sahara, shimmering and silent, while standing knee-deep in snow.

Fortified by bread and honey, cheese and a juicy or-ange, we made the final ascent.

It is said that the Atlas Mountains have no foothills to

speak of, and I could believe it. Standing on the fourteen-thousand-foot summit of Jebel Toubkal, surrounded by ice and snow and buffeted by a swirling gale, I was looking right down on the hot and dusty plain of Marrakesh, where the red city was faintly visible. There I was, poised on one of the tallest mountains in Africa, and there, scattered across a lesser peak, lay the wreckage of an airplane which had not flown so high.

June 1 - Dar Tounsi

The beekeeper in the forest. Weighing the honey, he asks M and me if we have seen any clouds lately. I tell him we haven't seen any in weeks. He hadn't seen any for years. We went away.

June 2 - Marrakesh

Adolfo de Velasco is one of Morocco's great hosts. Whether in his palace in the Tangier Kasbah or Les Jardins Majorelle in Marrakesh, he entertains on a vast scale. Candelabras six feet high, a mountain of oysters, a whole roast suckling pig, dozens of smartly dressed servants—the proportions are epicurean, something out of Rome or Hollywood.

When they're in town, YSL and Pierre Bergé always turn up at the Marrakesh affairs. Yves—worn out and oozing angst, moaning about the workload and wishing aloud he were an artist not an artisan. Business-like Pierre stands behind with his pitchfork, prodding the exhausted genius to greater efforts. Afterwards we went back to their house for a swim.

June 5

Irene Pappas, in Marrakesh shooting the film about the life of Mohammed, told me the story of her elopement. She was seventeen. She took a boat from Athens to Salonika. It was windy and raining. She slept on the deck, on a coil of rope. A soldier threw his coat over her. She had with her two dresses—one silk and one cotton—which she had made herself, and one pair of shoes. She met her fiancé and they went to a hotel. When he left the room to take a bath in another part of the hotel, she hid under the bed, thinking to surprise him when he returned. (She was going to grab him by the ankle.) She stayed under the bed for an hour, counting the springs, but he did not return. Wondering what had happened, she went searching for him. She found him asleep in the bathtub. Wearing her only pair of shoes, she jumped into the tub with him, and they splashed the water making love. The next day she had to buy new shoes. The shoes made in Salonika were so crudely made (this was 1947) that men's and women's were indistinguishable. She and her husband could not tell their shoes apart.

Her mother is eighty. Whenever Irene visits her, her first question is always about her daughter's sex life. Not just general terms; the old woman wants to know all the fleshy details.

Casa Zugari, Calle Ajdir,
Merstakhoche, Tanger, Maroc.
22/v/74
Las once en punto

Dear John:

I send you many greetings. Friend John: It's very hot in here. Last Monday I had a big dream about you. I was asleep, and I saw you dancing with the Jilala, dressed all in white. And you were working with fire in your hands. There were a lot of English and Americans watching, and even some Moroccans, and they were all astonished. And you went on dancing with this burning tree-trunk in your hands, and you rubbed it over your face. Finally, when you finished dancing, I went up to you and asked you how you felt. You said: I feel as though I had been born yesterday. This is the true life, the way it should be. I got up and began to dance with a long knife in my hand. And there was blood everywhere. Everyone was afraid. Afterward, when I had ended the dance, there was neither blood nor a sign of a scar. You came and asked me how I felt. I said I felt that I was in Heaven. Then we laughed a great deal and I woke up. Amigo Hopkins, heat always feels hot, but fire can always be put out. If not with water, with earth. If not with earth, with green plants. If not with green plants, with a hard look. Thoughts are not the same. There are many people who believe what others say. And there are many others who don't. Amigo John, I want to ask you some questions, those questions I spoke about with you some time ago, and which you said you would answer.

First question: Why do you prefer Morocco as a place to live in, to the United States?

Second question: You've spent more than ten years in Morocco, much of it in Tangier, and some of it in Marrakesh. According to you, what are the best things in Tangier and what are the least good? And the same about Marrakesh.

Third question: Can you tell me why you want to travel across the Sahara on a camel by yourself?

Amigo John, the fourth question: I've noticed that you like the Jilala and also that you love to dance. Can you explain why you like to enter into the music of the Jilala? How do you feel when you dance?

Amigo Hopkins, life is very sad, and the world is very happy. And the sky is weeping, and the earth is drinking, and the sea drowning. The rocks are dancing and the trees are singing. The roses are screaming and the birds are moving. Amigo John, Paul and I are going to Marrakesh to spend a few days with you in your house in the oasis. In the year 1811, as you well remember, we were in Russia together; this was when we had been captured as spies and were in prison. The worms crawled out of our noses in that jail, and we sold them to the Russian soldiers to make tortillas with. Amigo Hopkins, don't forget the time you ate the donkey's ear and found it delicious. Amigo John, drink lots of well water, and take showers with well water, and you must travel a great deal and eat plenty and have many pretty girls. That is the world—enjoy oneself because death is at one's heels. Youth disappears and sicknesses arrive, and pains, and one is always tired. Amigo John, many thanks and gracias. Si quieres. Si no quieres, gracias. Adios, hasta Dios quiere. Buena suerte. Hasta pronto.

MOHAMMED M'RABET

[translated from Spanish by Paul Bowles]

June 25 - Melilla

This is Spain of the 1950s—quiet, with little traffic. The garbage wagon rolls on wheels six feet in diameter. Garbagemen in paramilitary uniforms. Legionnaires and *regulares* do the *paseo* with local girls. *Mucho pecho, poco macho*. The fishing fleet is moored in front of the Plaza de España, where tapa bars serve ice-cold beer beneath the old walls. Columbus made his third trip to America from here. *Hogar de pescadores*. Moroccans dominate the black market and money-changing racket.

June 28 - Carboneras, Spain

M and I are staying with my English publisher, Barley Alison, who has brought out *The Attempt* and *Tangier Buzz-less Flies* in London.

Ancient oyster shells the size of platters litter the hills behind this village. Indeed, the hills seem to be enormous mounds of crustaceous rubble, as close inspection of rock reveals a composition of compressed shell conglomerate. Colonies of pygmy owls inhabit dry river valleys and eroded cliff faces. Their shrill barking cries echo along the ravines. These stream beds were at one time intensely cultivated. Ancient fig trees are to be found, and the odd gnarled old almond or apricot; but now the land is the domain of owls, falcons and foxes. The goatherd chases off the predator eagle with the snap of his sling.

Saul Bellow is also staying. Poor guy, he can't get used to Spanish hours and wants his supper at seven, when most people in civilized Spain are looking at their first dry martini. He's like Bowles in this respect: whoever controls the food supply controls the writer. Walking to the beach we discussed Thomas Pynchon's *Gravity's Rainbow*. "He's a virtuoso," Bellow remarks, a bit testily. "I could write like a virtuoso, but virtuosos don't make good novelists. Technique and structure are required. The act of writing produces inspiration, not the other way around." Bellow, I think, secretly lusts after M and may be a little jealous of Pynchon.

July 2 - *High summer in Morocco*

Driving from Fez to Marrakesh in an open car we stripped to our underwear and poured bottles of Evian water over our heads. The shepherd boys screamed "Naked!" as we raced down the liquid road toward the heat-distorted horizon. When the sun goes down and coolness comes on, you feel you have survived the day and can begin to live at night.

July 4 - *Dar Tounsi*

"When desert-dwellers meet, they stand off a few paces to whisper sibilant litanies of ritual greeting, almost indistinguishable in sound from the rustling of stiff cloth, as they bare a long arm to reach out and softly stroke palms. They exchange long litanies of names interwoven with news and blessings until a spell of loosely knit identity is thrown over all the generations of the Faithful. . . ."

— *The Process*, B. Gysin

"Eternity flows all about us as we pull at my pipe, utterly silent under the stars."

— idem

"The staggering assumptions in my young companion's calm eyes. . . . There is no friendship in the desert, there is no love. The Sahara knows only allies and accomplices."

— idem

"The Sahara crackles with static electricity. . . . The desert dwellers are tuned in to the great humming silence. . . ."

— idem

July 6

Here in the palmeraie, removed from the lights of the city, night skies treat us to gaudy displays. Gigantic moons, shooting stars, wobbling satellites.

July 10 - مْرَاكْش

About two o'clock in the afternoon, the hot summer wind that the Moroccans call *el shergui* grabs you by the throat.

August 2

High summer. Dust storms and high winds every day. Thunderheads pile up in the afternoon. The wind carries the smell of rain, thunder grumbles, but the rain never comes. So hot it evaporates before it hits the earth, the Moroccans say.

August 6 - Tanja

Ellen Ann is back in town. We walked down through the eucalyptus forest (inhaling deeply) to Marguerite McBey's seahouse for birthday lunch (36 yesterday) and swim in the sea. In the evening we went to Malcolm Forbes' party on the Marshan, followed by drinks at the Parade Bar. At midnight we dropped in on Paul and M'rabet. (EA's playful bantering in Spanish always lifts the cloud from M'rabet's brow and that puts Paul into a happy mood.) At dawn we motored to Cape Spartel, drove across the wide beach, parked the car in the water, stripped and splashed through the welcoming waves that lap this North African shore.

August 11 - Dar Tounsi

Bill Willis is a magnet. The beautiful people don't come to Marrakesh to visit the Saadian Tombs or the Badi Palace. They make a beeline to Bill's amazing house in the medina at Zaouia Sidi Bel Abbess behind Bab al-Khemis.

August 18

Few flies this summer: those that are about move slowly. They can be swatted easily.

September 8

Last Saturday I returned late from one of Bill Willis' rooftop parties in the Marrakesh medina. As I entered the mud courtyard the car headlights picked up a tigersnake slithering along the wall.

Fearing the snake would climb the Liane de Floride and get into my bedroom, I jumped out of the car, picked up a hoe and chopped it in two.

Next morning I found my gardener Ahmed looking at the carcass and dismally shaking his head. The snake had a useful purpose, he explained. For many years it had lived in the palm trees around the house and kept the rat population under control.

I thought no more about it until Tuesday when something heavy dropped onto my bed in the middle of the night. I switched on a flashlight and glimpsed a rat as it jumped away. All that night rats were running through the house. The windows were open and La Petite Maison was full of them.

On Wednesday Ahmed and I drove to town and bought big ugly metal traps with teeth. He baited them with fresh bread moistened with a drop of olive oil and placed them on the windowsills.

That night there were loud clankings as the traps claimed their victims. Rats that had not been killed instantly could be heard dragging the traps about. Over the next two nights more than twenty were caught.

My nights became peaceful again, and I thought the crisis had passed. Then last night, groping my way to the bathroom, I shined my light on the walls to discover the place was swarming with cockroaches. They were pouring up through the drain. The rats had lived on cockroaches. I'd found a nest behind the stove and it was littered with cockroach wings. Now the rats had gone, the cockroaches had multiplied by the thousand!

I sprayed the place with bug killer and this morning we carried them away by the bucketful.

December 1 - New York

I've come to America with Madeleine to visit the family, to see Peter Matson, my literary agent, and to help Joe Pinto organize a fund-raising party for the American School in his fabulous apartment in the Dakota Building on West 72nd Street.

December 3

Dinner with Bill Burroughs in his loft on 77 Franklin Street. His secretary, James Grauerholz, cooked supper. Also there was Paul Getty III, missing one ear. Bill proudly showed me his fur-lined Wilhelm Reich orgone box where he spends several hours each day hoping to revive his creative powers.

December 15 - Paris

Last night Brion Gysin and I had our reconciliation, softened by offerings of a cashmere sweater from Harrods and a bottle of sour mash. Sick with cancer, Brion's body has aged, and he moves slowly. He has become old, like Burroughs. He has allowed his hair to grow long and now resembles an old woman which, he says, is exactly the way he wants to look. I am reminded of Proust's description of Charlus. The mind, however, has not lost its sharpness. We're here to go. He's convinced of this.

Brion on Peter Matson: "His hair's too long, he smokes too much pot, he sees too many chicks, he rides a bicycle—everything's wrong with him."

December 23 - Tangier

When Farooki has a stone in his mouth he's content. He doesn't bite people or other dogs. It must be a great big stone.

When he drops the stone, he goes for the ankle. "Give that dog a stone, please, he makes me nervous." A heavy dog with huge, dull teeth.

1975

January 12 - Dar Tounsi

Madame Zézé, proprietor of my favourite restaurant, is dead.

Mr. Zézé told me: "We ate lunch and played cards afterwards. I went off to the garage. When I came back about four, she was in the tub. I called to her not to stay in too long and to dry herself well afterwards, as she had a cold. (I could see her head through the half-open bathroom door.) When I came back an hour later she was still in the tub. The water had run out. She was forty-nine years old."

February 8

Oum Khaltoum is dead. All Morocco is sad. In the medina, radios broadcast her songs. Men with dreamy, melancholy expressions go about humming their favourite tunes. They are all hers. The Arab world wears a long face.

March 10 - On the bus between Zagora and Marrakesh

Sitting next to me is a boy who goes to school in M'hamid. I ask, after M'hamid, will he go to the secondary school in Ouarzazate? He says yes. Then I say, after Ouarzazate, Marrakesh? He nods. Then I say, after Marrakesh, the University in Rabat? Yes. After Rabat, Paris? He nods. After Paris, the United States, New York? He nods. Then I say, after New York, M'hamid. The men roar with laughter. "*C'est la vie*," sighs the fellow across the aisle. A crescent moon hangs over the desert as dawn comes on.

March 21 - Dar Tounsi

Paul and Abdelouahaid Boulaich have been staying for a week. They drove down from Tanja in the old bronze Mustang. Every morning Paul works on the M'rabet translations. After lunch we go for a drive. We have visited the cactus farm, lunched in the Ourika Valley, and had dinner chez Bill Willis. Every night we listen to Paul's tapes and talk about writing.

April 7 - Málaga. Looking for Jane Bowles' grave.

At Joe McPhillips' insistence, he, Mohammed Anakar and I are trying to find Jane Bowles' grave. This is proving to be much more difficult than we had imagined. La Clínica de Reposo de los Angeles, Arroyo de los Angeles, where she died two years ago, does not answer the telephone. We have spoken to the two big public cemeteries, San Rafael and San Miguel, but they are unable to help us. How can they consult their records if we don't know the date of the *señora's* burial? According to Paul, Jane, who was Jewish, was converted to Catholicism the year before her death, when she was already blind and had lost the power of speech. The nuns told her that there was no place in Malága for her to be buried except in a Catholic cemetery, as a Catholic.

We have finally got through to the Clínica. The sister informed us that Señora Bowles died May 4, 1973, and was buried at San Rafael. She could not recall, however, if she was buried the same day or the next. Jane was buried in the ground, the sister made a point of adding, and not in a wall, where the Spanish are generally entombed. Moreover, her grave was marked only by a provisional wooden cross.

We have telephoned San Rafael once more, but they are still unable to find any record of her interment, either May 4 or May 5. So we will drive out there this afternoon and have a look for ourselves. Like everything else in Málaga, the cemeteries are closed during the siesta hour. And the day is unseasonably hot.

What with the suburban sprawl and high rise apartment buildings going up everywhere, we drove around for an hour before we found San Rafael. We wondered how we could have missed it, there was so much going on. Automobiles, people on foot, even buses were arriving and departing. The incessant bustle and profusion of fresh flowers in the bright sunshine created a pageant-like atmosphere. We searched through the heavy ledgers where new entries were constantly being made, but to our consternation we could not find Jane's name. Discouraged and somewhat bewildered, we decided nevertheless to drive back across Málaga to the San Miguel cemetery, located on a hill overlooking the city.

This time we were able to find the cemetery by following the long line of women dressed in black who were filing through the streets. And Jane was listed in the book. We were given a scrap of paper with a number on it.

453-F

Great banks of flowers had been arranged on either side of the gate. We bought bunches of *claveles*. *Flores para los muertos*, so wrote Jane's friend Tennessee Williams in *A Streetcar Named Desire*. There was a café named San Miguel in the square outside the gate. Old men sat on the roots of a shade tree, leaning on sticks and waiting. We went in.

The vast cemetery was literally paved with graves. Those who weren't buried in the ground were entombed in high walls that looked a lot like those new apartment buildings going up everywhere. As Mohammed says, "In Málaga, everything is apartments."

There was a tremendous amount of activity. The cemetery swarmed with mourners. A squad of gardeners in blue uniforms was perfunctorily collecting rubbish and chopping weeds. Another profusion of flowers, both real and plastic, adorned the thousands of graves and tombs. Women in black were arriving in droves, carrying pails and brooms and more flowers. All about us, as we wandered uncertainly through, they were busily scrubbing and brushing the white-tiled tombs of the departed, planting fresh flowers and watering them, or just resting in the shade of the cypress and eucalyptus trees.

It took a long time to find Jane's grave. In the end, one of the gardeners led us to it. It was lower than the others because there were no tiles; there wasn't even a cross. Only a stick with a number on it. 453-F. We stood around and stared at it for a while, clutching our flowers. The brief moment of satisfaction at having found it was quickly swept away by the realization of what we were looking at: Jane Bowles' unmarked grave. It had become the refuse dump of broken flower pots and bottles and dead stalks cast aside by the assiduous ladies in black.

I'd known Jane since 1962—five years after her first stroke. The last time I had seen her had been in the summer of 1968, at the Clínica. The nun had led her out, and we had sat for an hour on the terrace. She had seemed numb or drugged; her speech had been disjointed and halting but coherent. We'd talked about Paul, and she had asked after Joe and Marta Ruspoli and other friends in Tangier. She looked terrible and knew it. Her shaggy appearance was a great embarrassment to her. Although she still had five years to live, her life was already over. There would be no more cats or parrots to keep her company or toy telephones to talk to Paul through; no couscous or jugged hare, no lentils or chicken à la king; no more domestic dramas or Moroccan theatre; and no friends. The zany hats and broken mirror were gone forever. She would never write again. She must have welcomed death and even prayed for it.

We were wondering what to do with our flowers when a little blue-eyed, thick-legged Spanish girl appeared out of nowhere and cheerfully volunteered to tidy up the grave area for us. While we watched, she scratched around and fetched water in a plastic bottle. When she had done, Joe gave her 25 pesetas, then 5 more, because Jane, alone in an unmarked grave among so many strangers, would have been touched, as we were, by the attentions of the little girl. It was a character she herself might have created—thick legs and all. The plot looked neater when she was through, but when the stick is kicked over and the number fades, and when the refuse begins to pile up again, it will be as difficult to find.

April 12 - Tangier

The bee-eaters are flying. They never seem to rest. They were Veronica's favourite bird. . . . Tennessee must have invented them.

April 13

The story of the monkey and the dog.

They lived on a farm outside Tangier. The monkey who took care of the puppy was frightened of the horsemen who rode past the farm. Every time he heard the sound of approaching horses, he carried the puppy to the top of the fig tree. The years passed. The puppy grew into a large dog, the monkey became older and weaker, and the tree grew to a great size. Now, when horses approach, the monkey leaps on the back of the dog and rides him up into the branches of the tree.

April 15

I asked her not to open the gate, but she did it anyway. I didn't want her to let loose that pack of baying hounds.

I wanted her to open the gate just a crack so I could slip through without dogs escaping. But she flung the gate wide open, and out plunged that mob of dogs, led by a team of powerful boxers to attack Joe's dog Kiang, the Chow. Nine dogs against one, and they were killing him there in the dark. A seething mass of snapping growling canines going for the throat. Kiang backed against the wall and defended himself as best he could with his jaws and thick, protective fur. His fur coat saved him. In the melee I was down on my hands and knees, vainly pulling the dogs off him. My hands and fingers were bitten and my arm chewed, right through my tweed jacket, at least once by Kiang himself. I was snarling and snapping with the best of them. It was a return to the Stone Age, when growling pre-men confronted wild beasts. I bit one boxer on the neck; it was like chewing on leather. I seized Kiang and attempted to lift him above the brawl, but the boxers hung on like crabs, and I was unable to kick them away. The fight lasted three or four minutes, but it seemed like a lifetime. Help arrived in the form of a night watchman with a cudgel. The dogs were finally kicked and beaten off. The two of us—Kiang and I—lay panting and bleeding against the wall.

Today my arms and hands are sore. I hold this pen with difficulty. And Mohammed, the one who came to our rescue, has dreamt of bubbles foaming from my mouth. Kiang was bitten many times but seems to have survived. He, too, is stiff and sore. We both walk with several limps.

April 27

Paul Bowles sits in his dark apartment with no telephone, yet he seems to know what's going on everywhere. I show him a book I've just received from NY; he's already read it. I can't wait to tell him some spicy bit of gossip, but he's already heard it. How does he do it? How does he stay in touch? The Arab telegraph?

May 2 - Dar Tounsi

Back here again. This journal is like the hole a dog crawls into when sick. Away from the noise and light, he sinks into semi-somnolence and waits for the pain to go away.

Reluctantly, I've put aside the short story I've been struggling with. Here there is no pressure, no anxiety. I simply put down the words as they trickle out. Ideas recorded here do no violence to my soul. The storm of anxiety has temporarily subsided. How sweet the peace is.

July 10

Hot here: 115° in the shade. Thermometers explode if placed in the sun. Killed a tarantula night before last. With the sole of a flexible leather sandal, one can deliver a hard, flat blow. Next week M and I go to Tangier where the flies don't bite, and where I won't have to go running to the shower every 15 min. to cool off.

July 11

Paul told me about an American tourist couple standing in front of him at the cornflakes counter at the Fez market. He (swatting violently), "These flies are driving me crazy!" She (irritably), "I bet that was another one of those blasted Tangier buzzless flies!"

July 25 - Tangier

The *poniente*, or *rharbi*, or west wind has been blowing for a week now. Days are dry, limpid and warm, halcyon days, the evenings quiet and cool. Ideal climate for anyone wishing to create. I sit in my tower overlooking the Strait of Gibraltar without a thought in my head.

September 5

"The beauty of this country is dependent upon its poverty." I forget who said that.

September 10 - Marrakesh

Bill Willis' rooftop party for Rudolf Nureyev. After dinner the musicians appeared, and N. treated the guests to an impromptu dance the likes of which they never saw at Covent Garden. He teetered drunkenly along the edge of the parapet. (We were four storeys up.) For a minute I thought his prodigious leaps would carry him onto the roof of the neighbour's house. Pretty soon everyone got into the act. Burt Lancaster sat on a pouf, grinning like a Cheshire cat. He trained as an acrobat and admired N's Superman jumps.

September 28 - Oualidia

Strange and protracted dreams beset me on this coast. How I sleep! A two-hour siesta, in which I float fathoms deep, plus ten hours at night, in the depths of turbulent dream waters. I wake feeling I've drowned.

A deep swell flows against this shore. The cliffs resound with thuds, geysers erupt, and the rocks bleed white water. Salt spray fills the air. I breathe well here—antiseptic, dust-free sea air has always benefitted asthmatics. At dusk, the lagoon and coastal depressions begin to fill with salty mist as we sit down to oysters, lobsters and fish, all washed down with gallons of white wine. Madeleine keeps no regular eating habits. Like an African lioness, she can go for days without food; but when presented with the kind of dish she likes (seafood is her favourite), she gorges herself.

December 10 - Dar Tounsi

The olive pickers are making a mess of the job. . . . It is icy cold. Deep snow covers the Atlas, and I don't feel happy about anything. Love has cooled, and departure from this mud house in the oasis seems inevitable. . . .

1976

January 1 - Marrakesh

Overheard in an Italian restaurant: "Now how much would a good-looking boy like me cost in New York?"

January 29

Zeitoun, asleep in front of the fire, howls in his sleep, waking me from my own nightmare.

April 2 - Rabat

Morocco in springtime. Shepherd boys on the Marrakesh road collect wild flowers, weave them into stupendous bouquets and wave them at passing motorists. Intimate association with nature brings out the artist in man.

April 8

From Plutarch: "Batalus, a certain enervated flute player, meagre and sickly, a writer of wanton verses and drinking songs. And it would seem that some part of the body, not decent to be named, was at that time called the Batalus by the Athenians."

April 10 - Dar Tounsi

The turtle doves have arrived early. And the rollers. Their turquoise wings flash in fancy flight, but they converse in hoarse croaks.

April 29 - Tangier

Where there are more shoeshine boys than shoes.

June 4

"The human soul knows that growth is the only reason for its existence." S. Bellow.

August 24

Celine's biography reminds me of Pound—the romanticism, the despair, the fascist propaganda, the anti-semitism. Celine despised the Mediterranean and embraced Hitler. Both writers hated the world, or what was happening to the world, the way they thought the world was going. Both sought solutions for the world . . . and for their relentless pessimism. Both suffered from arrogance. Their solutions are boring, vicious, repetitive. Both were famous for their imaginative works. Both were iconoclasts who developed new styles that shattered the old. Despair goaded their pessimism. Both were rebels. Both miscalculated. Both suffered from poor judgement.

October 6 - Tangier

8 rue Brooks is my new address, or 8 ex-rue Brooks, re-named 8 Ibn Zaidoun. Brooks, an Englishman, planted trees in Tangier; Zaidoun, I am told, was an Arab poet.

M and I have split up. I have left my mud house in the oasis and returned to live in a modern apartment in Tangier, in order to be among friends.

October 7 - Tangier

Today, lunch with Dr. Pierre Parodi whom I have not seen since June 1971, when M and I drove from the Tantan *moussem* to Tata in the Moroccan desert. He has returned to the community of L'ARCHE, in southern France, where he no longer works as a doctor but as a farmer, with his hands. Bald, spare, wearing a loose white shirt, he eats little, drinks water, but will smoke one cigarette (Craven A) after lunch. He is vegetarian, I believe, or principally a vegetarian, and knows a great deal about grains, upon which he largely subsists.

We spoke about Tata; he is on his way there for a 20-day visit. A French agronomist (M. Tutu, Tuti?) in Marrakesh has made a seven-year study from which he concludes that a Saharan (sedentary) family of eight can subsist wholly and comfortably upon one hectare of land, providing, of course, that the land receives an adequate supply of water. Some two hundred palm trees will be planted, ten meters apart, and the land will be tilled. Vegetables, barley, etc. Room will be provided for a cow; fodder will be grown for her. There will also be six sheep and some goats, plus a little extra land (the plot is actually somewhat larger than one hectare) which can be sold for cash. So.

L'ARCHE, which comprises some one hundred souls, possesses 400 hectares of land. However, much of this land is not arable, and there are rocky areas and forests, just south of the Massif Central not far from Bezier. Dr. Parodi speaks of L'ARCHE, as he does of every subject, with a straightforward but not somber seriousness. One guesses he likes a good laugh and has an eye for the comic side to life. We ask about drugs. There is no drug problem at L'ARCHE. The children are involved in every activity; they are aware of every problem at L'ARCHE. There is no division of people by age, and everybody, be they grandfathers or children, does the same thing. Not like the children in the cities these days, he maintains, where people lead narrow, stratified lives defined by age, occupation, income, interests, etc. One gets the impression from Dr. P. that L'ARCHE is a fully integrated society, in the desert sense. He is questioned about industrial societies. He shakes his head. He is interested, however, in "Sufi technology"—solar energy, windmills, etc. Yes, that is of great interest to him.

One feels that here is a man of broad equanimity. When he speaks of the desert, L'ARCHE, or Tangier, the tone never varies. Here is a man who never acts out of character. If he is a man of surprises, and I am not saying that he is not, the surprises would probably derive from depth, not variance.

He speaks of his children. In Tata they learned the Berber language easily and fluently. As a result, they saw the world differently, they gained another perspective on the inhabitants of the Tata area, through their language.

Everywhere in the countryside, he maintains, people are bored. The countryside is dead, there is nothing to do. *Ils s'embêtent.* So they migrate to the cities and enter the narrow, stratified life. L'ARCHE, I assume, presents a deliberately maintained example that life doesn't have to go that way. As for food, the community is totally self-supporting. They even make some of their own clothes.

During lunch Joe was worried that his Rolex had been stolen; as he left, Dr. Parodi spotted it in a shoe by the front door.

October 16 - At the tennis court,
Emsallah Gardens, Tangier.

Pert, pretty, smartly dressed Moroccan girls, seventeen or eighteen years old, greet one another with exquisite tenderness. They exchange kisses, whisper intimate greetings and smile sweetly, all without the slightest trace of sincerity.

October 18 - طبخـة

At Villa Gazebo, when I ran out of ideas, I used to sweep the terrace. At the Petite Maison in Marrakesh, the sight and sound of water running in the irrigation ditches induced in me a fresh mood of thoughtfulness. Here on rue Brooks, when I can't think what the next sentence will be, I grab the Chinese fly-swatter and stalk bugs that have gathered on the windows and ledges.

October 31

Tangier has been hit by torrential rains, as one thunderstorm after another bursts upon the Barbary shore and sweeps down the Strait. Streets have become rivers. The drains, instead of sucking in water, regurgitate it in foaming fountains. Mud oozes from building sites; it spreads like lava across streets, making them impassable to all but joyous, naked children. I am told two women drowned in Beni Makada when their house filled with water.

The tides have torn up beaches, and new rivers flow across the sands. The sea around this northwesterly hump of Africa has turned a brownish-gray colour. The hills of Morocco, meanwhile, have taken on a greenish corpselike pallor. A few miniature wild flowers are blossoming in this, Tangier's annual autumnal spring. The whole country has slumped beneath the weight of water.

November 14

The blind vendor of lottery tickets staggers down the street:

"¡Un millón! ¡Un millón!" he chants.

He's filthy and dressed in rags. He holds his arms out in front of him (cane tapping). The lottery tickets are pinned to his sleeves and across his breast like a row of battle ribbons. There is no order to them; they are all mixed up.

"¡Un millón! ¡Un millón!" His voice is like the distant croaking of frogs.

November 16

In Morocco one stays in touch with the world the way it used to be: more beautiful, more diverse, less mechanical, less crowded, cleaner, safer and poorer.

November 27

Carla has returned from Afghanistan, where she had this dream:

Joe, Carla and I are standing at the edge of a vast lake in a frozen landscape. Beyond the lake are the "Chinese Mountains." The ground is as hard as rock, there's not a cloud in sight, the sky is blue, and the air rings with cold. Joe steps forth upon the lake. The ice is at least a foot thick and dark blue, almost black. He walks far out while Carla and I stand on the shore watching. Suddenly, unbelievably, despite the great thickness, the ice begins to give way. It breaks up slowly and Joe sinks from sight, spinning, arms flying, without a sound, without a splash. The water receives him soundlessly, like oil.

Carla is screaming "God! God! God!" She cannot (for some reason) look right or left. She doesn't know if I've run for planks or dogs. Then she woke up, her heart pounding.

November 30

I am not going to dwell miserably on my inability to make progress. The latest novel has simply run out of gas. I just want to ask one simple question: What is wrong with me and why?

December 18

This afternoon, between violent storms, I went on one of my Fundador walks around Tangier. First stop: Romero's Restaurant on Calle Goya, where I feasted upon *gambas pil pil*, San Miguel and *The Herald Tribune* while the Moroccans at the next table wallowed in red wine and *paella*. Then down Goya past the Rembrandt church, down the hill through the old Spanish quarter overlooking the harbour where, I was pleased to remark, many exotic gardens and villas bear the mark of care, maintenance, even habitation.

Emerging on the Avenida de España, I meandered beneath the double row of palms (presented to the city of Tangier by King Alfonso XIII), crossed the road and railroad to the beach, passing by the Ibn Batouta Restaurant, closed for the season and perhaps forever. There I found a tiny Moroccan bar and stopped for a second Fundador: 2 dirhams 50 centimes.

Sunlight raced across the bay as ephemeral sheets of blue sky shifted sideways. Soccer goals had been set up on the sand. A match was in progress, with seagulls floating. Several pious Moroccans prostrated themselves upon the sand as the soccer balls flew about. All was blue light as cumuli raced away toward the Pillars of Hercules.

The rain-soaked sand was firm beneath my feet. I felt like running or joining the game. At the Windmill, a beach bar, a Martel for 5 DH. Then back along the pavement past the new tourist hotels with clouds flying.

I wound up in the tapa bar Méditerranée, sipping my fourth brandy, watching soccer on TV. A drunken Moroccan approached; he knew my name. He loves America and insisted I listen to him recite the Preamble to the Declaration of Independence. He slurred the words, but they were all there, deep inside his heart.

December 25 - back in Dar Tounsi for a visit

These shining days. When depression strikes, I must remember this light reflecting off the snowy flanks of the High Atlas.

December 26

With M and my nephew Peter Clifford in Ouarzazate, where a new fountain splashes before every gas station.

December 27 - Tinerhir

The wind was blowing and Madeleine[1] was shivering. A heavy cold wind that swept down from the icy slopes of the Atlas. No resistance on the high plateaux in this stony, pre-Saharan region of the Moroccan south. M was shaking beneath the pitiless blue and white sky. She was running a fever. Her servant became alarmed. When she almost fell, he made her sit down and covered her shoulders with his burnoose.

December 28 - Dadès

Visited the gorges by car and oasis by foot. Picnicked on a stony ridge, far from the road, far from everything except the mineral silence that envelops this region. The oasis below the ridge was laid out and maintained with the spacious elegance of an English estate.

Ridge beyond stony ridge, where the stone breaks off in flat geometrical pieces ideal for building material. Moroccans came in trucks to rip the black rocks from the crumbling ridge. One sees the dry stone walls, fitted together with the tight combinations of a jigsaw puzzle.

The people of this region are gentle, tender, polite. They do not raise their voices except in prayer. Youths without jobs offer their services in an apologetic manner. Many young men are away in Holland and France, working in factories. They send their money back. Those without "contracts" have nothing to do and nowhere to go.

The gangs of itinerant and aimless young boys can be rambunctious. They inspire a little fear; but a polite response either neutralizes them or puts them off.

---

1. Madeleine van Breugel left Morocco in 1979. She later married and lived in Tanzania. On July 20, 1991 she died in Amsterdam of the fatal, flesh-eating disease known as Streptococcus A which she had contracted in Africa.

The Moroccans who inhabit this oasis:
>   they have little
>   they need little
>   they want little.

Their idea of luxury corresponds to ours of security: a steady job, food and clothes for the family, a roof that does not leak.

1977

January 5 - Sleepless in Casa

This city, whose population approaches two million, is as silent as a Saharan village in the middle of the night. Save for the crowing of cocks, not a sound is to be heard at four o'clock in the morning. A dog barks. This is the hour when the oasis re-enters the city. Stars shine down and a moon illuminates the black cobbled streets. (Square cobbles that give off a dull obsidian gleam under moonlight.) At 6AM trash fires flare in the empty lots as the homeless, wrapped in layers of djellabas and patched overcoats, beat their sides to warm themselves.

At dawn white facades brilliantly reflect the sun's first rays. Only now does the city deserve its name. The traffic consists mostly of horse- and mule-drawn wagons, laden with wicker baskets of fresh vegetables bound for the market. The wagons rumble over the cobbles, and the horseshoes ring and give off sparks. Casablanca, I imagine, is not unlike the Paris of the 1930s.

January 11 - Tangier

The combination of rainy weather, a cold coming on, an unresolved theft in my apartment, plus my inability to make progress on this novel has put me in a foul mood.

January 12

I've had a growth removed from my forehead. Dr. Anderson's clinic was so cold he insisted I wear my overcoat during the operation. Six stitches. The biopsy from

197

the Spanish hospital described it as a "proliferation of basal cells with long cords attached, and centered upon enormous horned globes!"

In other words, a wart!

January 15 - *Saturday morning in Tangier*

The young, good-looking but demented Spaniard walks along the sidewalk shrieking "Paloma!" His lonely voice can be heard for blocks. "Paloma! Paloma!" reverberates down the empty canyons of the boulevard.

January 16

The husky ex-wrestler, whom I saw perform years ago at Hasnona, has reappeared from the bowels of Dradeb with a deep crease cutting horizontally across his forehead. Like Frankenstein's scar but without stitches or electrodes. The eyes look down as he trudges along: the heavy unblinking stare at nothing. He, too, has gone mad.

But it's amazing how well-dressed the crazies in Tangier are these days. Mister Paloma had a flower in his lapel, and the ex-wrestler was wearing argyles (probably from the thieves' market).

January 18

Old Dr. Peñas, another refugee from the Spanish Civil War, whose raincoat collar is encrusted with dirt, and I encounter one another one rainy afternoon on Calle Holanda. We take cover beneath an awning, and the talk turns to lobsters. The night before a fisherman had turned up at Dr. Peñas's door, after dark because the hunting of lobsters is forbidden this time of year. The doctor scolded him for breaking the law, but the fisherman was persistent. "Look, doc, we're not going to throw the lobster back in the sea." Dr. Peñas finally bought the lobster and ate it, and it was delicious.

January 23

Rain. The African countryside is flooded; the hills have slumped and flattened their profiles from exhaustion, resignation and saturation. The roads have been gutted and battered; now they batter the automobiles. Tides of mud three feet deep make streets impassable. Houses melt and collapse; those attempting to escape drown in the night.

January 25, 1:35AM

Saturday night. A fight broke out on Calle Velasquez in front of the Bar Oriente Andaluz. The drunks tumbled onto the street, where they shouted and strutted, waved their fists, doffed their jackets and hurled them to the ground. They were restrained by other drunks and assorted peacemakers. They postured and pouted, and every now and then a blow was landed.

Someone called the cops. The police van arrived. The cops jumped out, grabbed everyone in sight, and hurled them tumbling into the van. One of their victims was a young *djibli* (mountain boy) in a knee-length djellaba. He protested when they pounced on him. He had been walking down the street and had nothing to do with it. Nobody vouched for him, naturally. In he went, kicking and shouting; he would keep the sullen drunks from the Bar Andaluz company in the klinker.

January 29

The stars are out; the moon is shining brightly; it is a peaceful North African night, full of shadow. The next minute the trees are bent over, the wind howls, and the rain drives along horizontally out of the sw. Suddenly it is all over. The storm has passed as smoothly as a symphonic movement. Stars twinkle, the moon races free of the clouds and wanders in a clear sky. All is quiet but for the sound of water running everywhere. Some nights three, four, or a dozen of these storms douse Tangier before plunging down the Strait toward Gibraltar.

January 31

Old Mr. Guitta, bitter after his best friend died: "Next to death, everything is emptiness and humbug!"

February 2

Ezra Pound: "Genius . . . an inevitable swiftness and rightness in a given field."

"Human greatness . . . unusual energy coupled with straightness, the direct shooting mind."

Talking about himself of course.

February 3 - طنجة

Seated in the recesses of the Café Central on the Zoco Chico is an emaciated, almost senile young man who only a few years ago was a student at the Italian School. His hair has turned white, his complexion is gray, he dresses in a long black overcoat that looks like a shroud. The necktie, however, looks as though it comes from Hermès.

February 5

The black she-goat, trailing a crimson ribbon of afterbirth, licks her new-born babe wobbling on tiny legs. Half an hour later, the kid is lustily nudging the swollen udder.

February 6

The child with a wash tub. "This is what we need," he says, thumping the side of the tub. "This is what we have." He points forlornly to the bottom of the tub where a few coins gleam.

February 7

The albino deaf-mute who stole an automobile. In the middle of the night he fell asleep on the horn waking the entire neighbourhood, and the police were called.

A few days later his body was found chopped into pieces: some say three; some say sixty.

February 9

Being a writer is like having a mistress who is eternally young. This seductress is capable of fulfilling all your fantasies. She brings forth your power; sometimes you can go all night. She makes you drunk; she likes to hear you talk dirty; and she laughs at all your jokes. The experience can be so intense that you leave your desk with a post-creative sensitivity akin to penile rawness; you don't want anybody to touch or talk to you until you can be alone for a while and unwind.

She's unpredictable, and just when you're in the mood for love, she'll contrive to make you feel depressed, frustrated, suicidal, an utter failure. Your hectic relationship derives from her complete mastery over you and your life. She's a sadist who cunningly contemplates your masochistic tendencies. Like any mistress confident of her charms, she demands constant attention and uses up all your time.

February 20

Clouds passing over Tangier turn sulphur yellow, apricot, peachy in the evening glow from the city.

February 27

As one grows older one becomes adept at turning off painful thoughts the instant they occur.

For example. "I am not writing." I avert my face and

shut tight my eyes as though I am about to be slapped yet manage, through some kind of mind clamp, to ward off the blow. I open my eyes, and my face resumes its normal shape.

February 28

Green is the colour of Allah; it is also the colour of hope.

March 2

Taxi driver with a sigh: "Tangier, alas, does not prepare one for the world."

March 3

The new band in from the mountains plays to an empty café. The waiters sit at tables with their hands over their ears. The owner is at the beach.

March 4

A grotesque indolence has come over me. I hang around the apartment, doing nothing, and spend a great deal of time in bed—morning, noon and night. This novel has ceased to interest me; I have arrived at the point of abandoning it altogether. It seems all wrong. I don't know what to do.

March 5

Joe maintains that my most profoundly creative bursts of energy have been preceded by a prolonged adventure into asceticism. Maybe so, but I don't feel like a desert trip right now. Aside from writing I don't know what I'm interested in, and I can't write. All great novels have deep roots, and I'm not sure where mine are. In such moments of desperation I always return to this journal. The act of recording my anxieties on paper invariably helps to relieve them.

March 6

This afternoon Paul comes for tea and to give his verdict on the piece I have written about searching for Jane's grave in Malaga.

March 7

Spring—Oum Erbiyaa or "Mother of Grass"—is here. I went swimming this afternoon, and jogged on the beach until some tourists arrived.

March 14

I don't understand what's happening to me. One day it's a case of nerves, my stomach's full of butterflies, and I feel close to tears. My sleep is beset by dreams so intense that the night seems like one long day, interrupted by a few short, unhelpful naps. I wake exhausted and stagger to the aspirin bottle. Have I lost my nerve and become hypercritical of my work? Here, when I should be at the height of my powers, I accomplish little. Moreover, I read little and go back to bed as many as four times a day, lying on my back with my hands behind my head, staring like a prisoner at the ceiling. I feel disgusted with myself. The only thing that offers relief is swimming in the frigid sea.

March 15

Something is wrong with me. Last night, listening to Joe read the poetry of Williams, Pound, Ransome, e e cummings and Auden made me understand one thing very clearly. The vision that provoked each of those poems I lack. The integrity that made those poems rock hard eludes me.

March 17

This is the third or fourth day I have been laid low by a

mysterious fever. It is now ten AM and I feel quite well, despite persistent pain in my lower back. If this day follows the pattern of those that preceded it, I will stay cheerful until noon, when the temperature rises and the malaise sets in. By bedtime the temperature will be near 40°, and the back pain excruciating. I will take a Veganin suppository and feel better in minutes—almost euphoric, in fact. I sweat quantities while asleep. Last night I went through four T-shirts and two pairs of pyjamas. The sheets and pillows are soaked; I wrap myself in towels. Today the doctor comes.

April 1 - *The Princeton Club of New York*

When my sister rang me in Tangier, urging me to come to America to visit the family, especially my father who has not been well, I jumped at the chance to absent myself from the fruitless task of writing.

April 2

On a Fifth Avenue bus: a pale blond girl about twenty-five years old was sitting beside her boyfriend. She was dressed entirely in white—white coat with white fur collar, white boots, gloves and hat. An element of sadness and resignation marked her face, a touch of the lost. Her choice of clothes accentuated the paleness of her skin. The only touch of colour was a pale pink scar running from ear to ear beneath her chin. She and her boyfriend were talking about it. She did it herself.

April 13

A heat wave has hit New York, the temperature is in the 90s, and the citizens mob the streets practically naked. Breasts and buttocks are unblushingly displayed. People dress aggressively in the flimsiest, most transparent garb. Some of the fleshy sights are dazzling; others make you want to turn away. . . .

April 14

Burroughs' residence at 222 Bowery is a derelict YMCA. Following his instructions, I called from a gas station across the street so he could come down, undo the chains from the door, and shoo away the panhandlers who sprawl across the steps. His "boardroom" is a wide, low-ceilinged area adorned with Gysin desert scenes. His secretary James Grauerholz did the cooking. Burroughs wanted to hear the gossip from Tangier. He was particularly eager to know what Bowles was up to. When I needed to take a leak he pointed to the men's room. There was a row of a dozen urinals to choose from.

April 19

The N.Y. subway is a refuge for individuals on the edge of sanity. The train roars in, and a muscular fellow in a yellow lumber jacket begins to shake all over. When the train leaves (he has not boarded it), he relaxes. The express train passes and he twists violently left and right, as though his spine is an axis and he is suspended by the neck from the limb of a tree.

The wooden gait of an alcoholic. The capillaries burn; the cheeks are orange. The soul of a city is to be found in its subway.

April 23

This evening, following a weekend with Priscilla and Geoffrey Wolff in Vermont, I asked Ellen Ann Ragsdale to marry me and . . . she accepted!

April 28/29 - Paree

A long evening with Brion Gysin, who seemed stronger

and much recovered since my last visit (Dec. '74).

"Constant pain is easier to live with. It's there all the time; you know it will never go away; you make up your mind to live and work and go on, until you die."

The evening began at his flat at 135, rue St. Martin, opposite the Beaubourg. Liverwurst spread on Jewish onion bread, washed down with Jack Daniels. We taxied to a progressive jazz club behind the Pantheon (a narrow street, a profusion of Greek restaurants) to listen to Brion's lyrics that had been set to music.

We waded through dark and narrow streets to the river. A curiously meandering walk. We peered at menus and couldn't make up our minds. Brion did not seem to know where he was going (not that he was in a hurry or lost) or what he wanted to do next. He led me, finally, to a stuffy and crowded Chinese hole in the wall. I was put off at first, as I had been by the jazz, and doubted the meal would be a success. Once more I was mistaken, and we devoured one steamed delight after another, each course no larger than a single mouthful.

Then to Boul Mich for café and calvados. Several. Many. Walking, walking we returned to his flat, where we stayed up talking until 3AM and we polished off the sour mash. I walked back through dawn-filled streets to the Hotel Angleterre on rue Jacob feeling high and happy that Brion and I are still friends.[1]

April 30

It's finally beginning to sink in: I'm going to get married!

May 11 - Tangier

Back in my old bed in the Gazebo tower, watching the

---

1. Brion Gysin died in Paris in 1986; his ashes were scattered on the sea from the Caves of Hercules, near Tangier.

hawks.

A glass of warm coffee soothes the nerves. Like Proust, I breathe easier as caffeine partially relieves my asthma.

May 12

Jim Wyllie, upon being asked about the health of his 94-yr.-old friend, Clough Williams Ellis: "The other day he was crossing the street in Port Merion when the handle of a passing motor car caught his coat pocket, and he was dragged for half a mile. Upon being told that he would have to spend a fortnight in a dark room to recover from a severe concussion, he stomped out of the hospital declaring that a good shake-up was just what he needed and he felt better for it."

May 13

Alec Waugh,[1] to substantiate a claim of residency in Tangier against tax litigation in Saskatchewan, has purchased a plot in St. Andrew's Cemetery for 3 pounds 10 and 6 and has sent the Canadians a copy of the receipt.

May 16

Today was an ugly day; the sun set in the middle of the sky.

June 10

Ellen Ann and I are going to be married in Gibraltar June 24, followed by a church ceremony in Tangier the next day. Otherwise, I don't know what I'm doing. With this novel, I mean.

---

1. The brother of Evelyn Waugh and author of *Island in the Sun*; *Hot Countries*; *Love and the Caribbean*; *Loom of Youth*; *No Truce with Time*; *The Balliols*; *Married to a Spy*; *Fuel for the Flame*; *The Mule on the Minaret*; *My Place in the Bazaar*, and many other books.

June 24

Today we went to Gibraltar for the civil ceremony. Ellen Ann and I caught the early morning Gibair flight with Marjorie (Lady) Tweedale,[1] Helen Harrison,[2] Tessa Codrington[3] and Joe McPhillips. Ernesto, the Spanish cabbie, met us at the airport in his Mercedes and drove us to the registry office, where Mr. Flowers welcomed us. Helen was so overcome with emotion she couldn't sign her name. Ellen Ann had to hold her hand. Into the municipal garden for photos (Mr. Flowers informed us that he married Frederick Forsyth earlier in the year), then on to the Rock Hotel for champagne and caviar. Ernesto was with us the whole way, guzzling champagne, wolfing the caviar and snapping photos. Then back to the airport for the flight back to Tangier and a Jilala party at Villa Gazebo.

The wedding guests had arrived from Little Rock, Memphis, Far Hills, New York and London. My nephew Peter Clifford came from Montpellier in France. Even though we are officially married, Marjorie Tweedale, who is giving the reception, insisted Ellen Ann go to her house for the night. It would bring bad luck if the bride and groom sleep together the night before the church wedding. So I am alone.

June 25

I got up at seven not too hung over and drove to the Atlantic for a swim and a run on the beach. At ten Joe arrived and we walked, in our tropical suits, down Calle San Francisco (the blackened smithies shouted from their murky caves) and took a short cut through the market (the flower ladies handed us bouquets) to the church.

1. English resident in Tangier.
2. Friend of the bride from Little Rock, Arkansas.
3. Photographer and friend of the bride from London who inherited a house in Tangier.

There hasn't been a wedding in St. Andrew's Church for years, and *tout Tanger* was there. Ellen Ann had been drinking Bloody Marys with her bridesmaids at Madame Porte's until a half hour before the ceremony, but she managed to arrive at the church on time, on the arm of The Hon. David Herbert, who gave her away. Louise de Meuron arranged the floral headdress, and my bride carried a huge magnolia blossom from David's garden, symbolic of her southern heritage.

We were married by the Rt. Revd. Edmund Capper, Bishop of Tangier. The wedding was followed by a lavish reception at Villa Azul, Marjorie's home on Djemaa-el-Mokra. After the champagne had been drunk, lunch eaten, the cake cut, the bouquet thrown, etc., EA and I went home in the consular limo for a quick change of clothes. Then we raced in our own Renault up the mountain to the Gazebo to feast on baby lamb chops bought that morning by Driss Drissi at the roadside butcher in Souk-el-Arba. Then off to Abdu's "Caf" on the beach at the *Forêt Diplomatique*. In true Tangier fashion the Christian ceremony was followed by Muslim madness; the wedding guests danced to the Sufi beat until dawn.

June 27

"Death posts its challenge with a single gray hair." Arab proverb.

"الموت يعلن عن تحديه بخصلة شيب واحدة"

June 28

Everybody, it seems, needs someone to kick. On Calle Libertad in front of the Hotel Minzah the obsequious *guardien des voitures*, who bows when he puts his hand out and murmurs salaams while receiving a coin—he, too, has his whipping boy. We come upon him beating a child, probably his own. Teeth we never saw before were bared, long yellow fangs protruded, and the voice we had only heard as a whimper was now a rasping bark. The eyes blaze with malice, and the child, with reason, recoiled in horror. He did not cry out when the blows fell with venomous force, so great was his fear.

We wonder if this whispering, grovelling attendant, who addresses me as "*professeur*," yearns to administer the same fiendish punishment to all he serves.

June 29

Ellen Ann discusses fashion with our maid. Fatima's husband wants her to wear the veil above the nose, but she refused and wears it below the nose. Before she married she went out with nothing over her face. She also dislikes wearing the traditional djellaba and hood because they are too hot. She prefers to go bareheaded, but her husband forbids her to show her hair in public.

Now Fatima's sister-in-law is in the kitchen, waiting for Fatima to finish her work. Ellen Ann has just suggested they all have a cup of coffee. This is turning into a rehearsal for a Jane Bowles play.

June 30

Bint. *Bint diali.* بنْتْ دْيَالي = my girl.

As Geoffrey Wolff predicted, Ellen Ann has rescued me from the gloomies.

July 2

Sunday morning. We've been married a week now. The last wedding guest has departed, and today is the first we've had to ourselves. We stayed in bed until eleven. Fatima brought us hot *café au lait* with toast and honey. The sun is shining, and our *lune de miel* is just beginning.

We've come to this place to stay with our friends Driss and Khaltoum Drissi, also recently married. Driss went to the American School of Tangier and studied forestry at North Carolina State. His mother has sent an old aunt and uncle to wait on him and Khaltoum. The aunt does the cooking and cleaning. The white-bearded uncle (Papa Nöel) spends his time cutting kif and running errands for the young master. *Quel service!*

Yesterday I climbed up to Bab-el-Ars, or Gate of Pines, the only indigenous fir forest in Morocco. From the top of the mountain I had an incomparable view of the Mediterranean and the Rif. I had set out at 3:30PM and had not planned on going so far, even though Driss had often spoken of the forest. I'd had a huge lunch and was full of energy. After an initial stiffness in the calves due to the continuous uphill trek, I felt I could go on forever and did, all the way to the top. Another reason was that the path was smooth and clear nearly the whole way.

At one point, when I was edging along a cliff face (I had left the path), I spied a hundred feet below me a falcon's nest, where the young birds were screaming and squabbling. As I watched, a diving falcon raced past my ear with a woosh like a cannonball, and I felt the wind from its flight. The Andean Condor is known to knock a man from his saddle and feed on his remains at the bottom of the cliff, but I was surprised that a small falcon would employ such tactics. If he meant to scare me, he succeeded.

The columned forest was gloomy and cathedral-like. Shafts of light illuminated, with chiaroscuro effect, the corpses of the fallen. The eerie moan of wind through the branches did not make me feel at ease.

I began my descent and startled a solitary wild boar on the path. It made me anxious to get down from the mountain before dark.

At sunset those gray peaks reverberated with the whistles and shouts of the goatherds, the barking of their dogs and the cries of lost or stray kids. The noise made by rutting goats, impossible to describe, echoed fantastically across the valleys and chasms. They roared, whined, warbled, farted and sent rocks cascading in the continuous pursuit of sex. The billygoats' red dripping penises were extended, their balls were colossal, and the nannygoats' vaginas and teats were grotesquely swollen. The sexual organs of goats, it seems, are oversized, just as the noises of copulation were fiendishly excessive. No wonder the ancients portrayed the goat as the devil incarnate.

My absence had so alarmed Ellen Ann that she was about to organize a search party.

Driss had rented the local *hammam*, where we spent the evening being luxuriously massaged and scrubbed by a team of washers. Today legs, from toe to hip, are very, very sore.

July 22 - Tangier

The cab driver driven mad by people and heat. We stopped at an intersection to allow a line of tiny Moroccan schoolgirls, walking in pairs, to pass. He rolled down the window and shouted, "Whores!"

August 1

When Marguerite McBey hit seventy, she levelled off. Nobody can explain it, but she just stopped getting older. According to her friend David Herbert, she became a different person after her husband James died. Having lived under his strict, authoritarian regime, she shed her shy nature and blossomed into a successful artist. David compares her to a chameleon who crawls from the shadow of a leaf and surprises itself by changing colours in the sunlight. James liked to have tea and crackers at six o'clock and go straight to bed. Marguerite started giving dinner parties that went on until the early hours of the morning. She keeps her exact age a secret but has managed to arrest the process of ageing through the sheer enjoyment of life.

Marguerite has always painted, but only recently has her talent flourished. An accomplished watercolourist, she has a show every other year in New York or London. And she makes the best Bloody Marys in Tangier.

Dressed in black slacks, white ankle boots, and a loose-fitting terracotta-coloured blouse belted at the waist, she came onto the terrace to greet us newly-weds. (As a wedding present she is going to paint Ellen Ann's portrait.) A Moroccan manservant stood at a discreet distance.

Marguerite's skin was brown from the sun, and her black hair was swept back from her high, domed forehead and gathered in a tight bun behind her head.

An orange scarf was draped across her shoulders like a serape. Heavy pearl earrings had, over the years, tugged openings in her ear lobes. Large amethysts and pale emeralds in solid gold settings glowed on her fingers. A string of thick, irregularly shaped lumps of coral hung around her neck. The sheer size of these precious stones, combined with the primitive boldness of their settings, made me feel I was in the presence of a high priestess from an ancient tribe. Orange lipstick lent a modern touch, but it was the aura of mystery and timelessness (and happiness) that prevailed.

August 5

Wind from the east and a deep swell striking this rocky Barbary shore. My annual birthday party at Marguerite McBey's sea house. "The sea is washing its laundry today," says Hamid the cook as he fans the charcoal with a palmetto leaf. The waves spill suds over the rocks. Grilled sardines, salade niçoise, a broiling sun and bottles of cold white Moroccan wine.

After lunch we leap into "the sluice" where you have to swim for your life or the waves will sweep you against the rocks. You haul yourself out, body burning from the icy sea. A profound sense of good health and well-being convinces you that, if there is heaven on earth, it's to be found here in this northwest corner of Africa.

August 7

Last night the annual *moussem* at Sidi Kacem. A mist rolling in from the sea softened the light and made fuzzy all visible figures and forms. The scraggy, ancient olive trees waved like kelp in the mist flowing among them. The lanterns glowed like signals from deep-sea creatures swimming through the ooze. Boys had climbed trees to watch the Aissaoua dervishes dance on broken glass. The Jilala dancers bumped each other like boxers, and the crowd was deep, intense and immoveable.

The mist felt soft against my face. While the others remained in the grove, I sat on the sand near the entrance to the tomb on the top of the hill. Pilgrims were coming and going. A group of *tolba*, dressed in white, chanted for money. I loved the anonymity provided by the mist and wanted to stay for the night. Had I had a sleeping bag, a bottle of Oulmès, and Kraa to guard me, I would have happily closed my eyes. As it was, I listened dreamily to the sound of drums, as the young men home from Belgium gyrated violently, kicking up the dust.

One old Jilali, in deep trance, placed one bare foot and then another on the red-hot coals of a brazier. He put the coals into his mouth and spat them at the spectators. Driss's bride Khaltoum, who had never visited a *moussem* before, felt the tug from the Jilala drums and the eerie notes emitted by *shebaba* (a transversal flute). The urge so frightened her she ran away.

I wondered if Driss would permit her to dance.

To this question he replies that he would.

When Khaltoum or other adepts hear the music, they feel incomplete until they dance. The dance completes, the dance relaxes, the dance exhausts, the dance exorcises, the dance soothes, the dance reunites the pieces of their lives. Afterwards a wondrous sense of freshness is felt.

August 9

Malcolm Forbes' annual summer blast. The entrance to Dar Mendoub is guarded by a phalanx of gleaming motorcycles lined up like the praetorian guard. Young, muscular motorcycle mechanics and balloon experts, each dressed identically in a red shirt with the words "Capitalist Tool" written in one of ten different languages on the back, dart about trying to be helpful.

The house is so big a street runs through it. Drinks in hand, we wander about and take in the lead soldier and oriental art collections, and the myriad framed photographs of world leaders and famous people whose hands Malcolm has shaken. Our host is there greeting his guests. The genius of Malcolm is that he has time for everybody. Busy as he is, I have never seen him in a hurry. Tangier is happy to have him, and of course the whole town turns up at his parties.

Upstairs, it is rumoured, is a bathroom and rumpus room of gargantuan proportions that is strictly off-limits to guests.

After the party Dr. Anderson gave Ellen Ann and me a lift to the Parade in his lima-bean-green 1947 Plymouth. It was the first time I had ridden in it since those asthma attacks back in 1963.

August 12

Last night Ellen Ann dreamed that her mother had decorated the house with dead fish.

Louise de Meuron is living proof that the most interesting people in Tangier are those who appreciate Moroccan culture and interweave it with their own. She lives with her lover Ahmed on the edge of the Marshan overlooking Jew's River. The house is an extremely comfortable shoebox, but the garden spilling down the hillside is a semitropical paradise. Her food, served by Fatomah, a white negress from the River Draa, is the most succulent in Tangier.

With her squeaky patter of Arabic, French, Spanish, English and German, Louise runs her establishment with the efficiency of a Swiss hausfrau. Condemned to an insane asylum in Switzerland by her husband (by Swiss standards she was deemed crazy; by Tangier's she seems utterly sane), she managed to escape the Alps intending to visit her uncle in Indonesia. While waiting in Gib for the boat to Jakarta, she decided to take a day trip to Morocco. On the Tangier dock she spotted a handsome stevedore and never looked back.

Every year she throws a huge fancy-dress party for her children and grandchildren when they visit from Switzerland. The kids seem not at all fazed by their sexually active grandmother and her swarthy lover. A phenomenal swimmer, Ahmed takes them to remote beaches and gives them lessons in fishing and scuba diving.

The party takes place on an abandoned tennis court at the bottom of the garden. A huge bonfire is lit, and Moroccan musicians (Jilala and Gnaoua) provide the African beat. Banquettes are arranged as little rooms around the perimeter of the court. The scene is lit by the roaring fire, hundreds of candles, and huge flaming torches spaced down the mountainside to the sea. Colourful Moroccan lanterns hanging in trees produce a 1001-Nights effect. Guests in gaudy costumes are announced by a pair of

Moroccans blowing six-foot Ramadan horns. Drinks and food are served, and some bring kif or hash. Led by Abdullah the lighthouse-keeper, the children and their friends dance through the night.

I write this today because Louise has cancer, and last night's party will probably be her last.

August 25 - Ramadan

Eight o'clock is the mad hour, the hour before *harira*. A man ran amok in the market on rue de Fez brandishing a piece of sharpened wire, which he threatened to plunge into a fruit vendor's eye. A mob of vegetable merchants subdued him; then a fight broke out among them.

Tempers are short; the Moroccans are in an irritable mood. Policemen have been posted at the major intersections, but collisions occur anyhow, followed by posturing and cursing. Moroccans don't fight with fists; they butt with heads like goats. It's a dangerous moment to be on the road.

August 27

D. Herbert. "Nature lovers make poor lovers, you know. Their minds and interests are with the flowers and the animals. There is no passion left for us."

September 23 - Far Hills, New Jersey

Last night's dream.

A Bolivian mining community with wind howling across the *altiplano*. A miners' café on the edge of town. The Indian faces were jaundiced and shiny, not unlike the yellow ore they scrape from the earth. They listened impassively to my argument with the barman over a hamburger. The meat was red and inedible. He wanted to throw me out.

I did go out. In a depression on the plain a tent was

being set up. A travelling circus had arrived in a wagon towed by an elephant. There was difficulty erecting the tent in the cold wind which never ceased to blow.

September 24

Tonight my mother is throwing a big party in our honour—a big marquis has been set up on the lawn—but little happiness warms this household. Ellen Ann and I have stepped into a minefield of warring factions and family misery going back twenty years.

October 4

To take a piss in the woods at night evokes a thoughtful mood. Branches rubbing together in the wind produce a sound like the moaning of a tortured soul.

November 2 - Back in Tangier

This afternoon we drove Michael and Penelope Nettlefold[1] to the sea in the roaring mufflerless car.

These extraordinarily clear days occur perhaps six times a year in Tangier. The sea flat and ribbed with water lanes, the ships coming and going in peaceful sequence through the Strait . . . you could spit at Spain. We visited the Belvedere at Rmilat and the lighthouse at Spartel. Walking the Atlantic beach, wading barefoot and collecting shells softened the reality that Marjorie Tweedale is dying.

November 4

Today is a gloomy one, overcast, with the smell of rain as the wind shifted to the SW. I tried to raise the wooden blinds in the bathroom window, and WHAM! the strap broke and the blinds came crashing down.

While I labour on the book, Ellen Ann is on the tennis

---

1. Son and daughter of Lady Tweedale.

court, wearing my sweater, swatting balls with Hussein, working up a sweat and exhausting herself. She has even promised a protein lunch!

November 13

Crescent moon at dusk.

This afternoon I walked to Boubana Cemetery. Louise de Meuron lies buried at the top of the hill in a vacant meadow near the northwest wall. Her grave, too fresh to be marked by a permanent headstone, was piled with porous rock (suitable for millstones) from Cape Spartel where Ahmed likes to swim. Someone had left a bouquet of wildflowers.

I sat down and eventually fell asleep in the grass by the grave. When I woke, the air had chilled by several degrees. I walked back to town, rested and refreshed from my catnap among the dead. Stopping in a café at the foot of the Old Mountain Road for a glass of mint tea, I mused on the sobriety of Moroccan life, refused a pipe of kif, and decided that I would always count myself fortunate to have lived in Tangier.

The cold, meanwhile, had begun to grip my shoulders with an icy hand—*summura*—and I walked swiftly home.

November 14

I'm going to go on writing novels, I also decided over that glass of mint tea yesterday, to write what I must write and to live more simply and more austerely, no matter what anyone else wants me to do. In this department at least, I know best.

November 17

Today Ellen Ann and I accomplished more in conversation than I have in several days on paper. The liberating effect of dialogue as thoughts fly free.

219

Tonight . . . our friend, the man who married us, who blessed this marriage and blessed this house, Rt. Rev. Edmund Capper, comes to dinner with Paul Bowles, Joe McPhillips, Gavin Lambert,[1] and the actor Brian Bedford. David Herbert and friend will stop by for a drink before dinner.

November 21

Joe's dog Kiang died this morning. He awaits the results of the autopsy but believes it will show he was poisoned.

Kiang had been sick for several days and couldn't move. Then he appeared to improve; he walked a little and ate. Last night he took a turn for the worse: Joe thought he heard him fall downstairs (Kiang had been sleeping in the tower room, where no one would disturb him, since he had been sick). Joe found him in the kitchen, walking in circles and vomiting bile. He lay down on the tiles near the front door where it is cool. Joe checked on him an hour later, and he wagged his tail. Then this morning he found him cold and stiff. He had vomited again and haemorrhaged through the anus.

The silent and patient suffering of animals. They rarely cry out; they don't know how to complain. They lie still and rest, conserving their strength, and wait patiently for the sickness to pass, or for death.

November 24 - Thanksgiving Day

Marjorie Tweedale died in her sleep early this morning. As Isabelle Gerofi[2] says, each death is a catastrophe for Tangier. Another person disappears, another house closes,

---

1. Anglo-American writer living in Tangier. Author of *Inside Daisy Clover*; *The Dangerous Edge*; *The Slide Area*; *In the Night All Cats are Gray*; *Running Time*; *Norma Shearer*; *On Cukor*, and several film scripts. Now resident in Hollywood.
2. Manager of La Librairie des Colonnes, Tangier's leading bookshop.

and there is nothing and nobody to replace them.

November 26

Clear light and blue sky: the Strait appears to be covered with pale blue ice. Death is out there flying. Marjorie's soul swoops up into clear invisibility. I hope she's happier there than she was here.

November 30

Dreary gray rain continues to fall, staining and darkening the countryside. The pavement glitters as pedestrians scurry along. This morning on rue Goya I came upon Alec Waugh. Like a Charlie Chaplin figure, diminutive in a dark coat, he was struggling to open an umbrella in the pouring rain. After much feigned and polite objection, he accepted my own. He also invited me to retrieve it at noon and to accept a dry martini. He and his wife Virginia Sorensen pleaded with me not to be discouraged. They have just reread *Tangier Buzzless Flies*.

December 1

From the beach front the drenched city looks black and sodden. Thousands of gulls float near coastal steamers anchored in the bay to escape the storms. Long streamers of black cloud herald more bad weather. These wild nights are illuminated by hectic flashes of lightning. Low, rushing clouds are coloured orange and pink by the street lights. From time to time the city lights, reeling from another lightning bolt, blink and go out. The city is under attack by the elements! But now it will be clean.

How good it will be to bake my bones in the Sahara! To breathe the crystal air, to bathe in unobstructed light! We leave the day after tomorrow, but I feel that my famished soul has already fled down the long road south. My sluggish body must catch up.

Clear winter light illuminates the green North African shore in all its contours and lushness. The earth has been made soft by late November rains, and farmers are busy behind mixed teams of cows, mules and donkeys. Following the ploughs, cattle egrets tug fat worms from the freshly turned soil.

Ellen Ann made a quick dash into Spain (Ceuta) for Glenfiddich, black chocolate, *jamon serrano* and *chorizo*, so we are well stocked for the trip. I returned to Fnidaq to order bamboo chairs for our dining room. We met at the frontier and drove to Chauen, where we are happily and warmly ensconced in the Hotel Asmaa. (No relation to my affliction.) We have drunk the Glenfiddich with ice and a dash of Oulmès brought by the tall languid Abdelaziz, who wafts about in a long white robe, anxious to please. We have pushed the beds together, ordered more pillows and blankets, had our soup delivered, and are content to read and drink (EA has already fallen asleep) without leaving the room. The anonymity is pleasing. Few people know where we are. Having scaled it last summer, I visualize the mountain peak outside this window. The wind rattles the window panes but I feel safe. In order to rid myself of my cold and my asthma, I will forsake the temptation of the *hammam*, the café, the square. We're happy. She's sound asleep. My adorable wife makes the ideal travelling companion. She's free now—released from the heartache of Marjorie's dying. Our plan is to head south over the Middle Atlas to the desert, visit Erfoud and Zagora, returning to Tangier via Marrakesh in time for Christmas.

This is my last adventure before turning to the serious matter of re-embarking on the novel. This trip, I hope, in the company of my beloved bride, will release me for the work I'm anxious to get on with. She's adorable! I love her! I want to protect her!

December 4 - Sefrou

The rain is coming down, down, down. By mistake we took the farmer's track from Ouazzane, and for hours meandered through the unrelieved Moroccan farmscape, black and sodden with the rain. Here in Sefrou, however, luxury of luxuries, our hotel room is blessed with both heat and hot water! My wife suffers from a chest cold, sore throat and, I fear, incipient bronchitis. Happily, the hotel has supplied us with extra pillows and blankets, and she never complains.

How we both long for the Saharan sun! We wrap up warmly in woolly burnooses.

Sefrou is more French than I had expected, with tree-lined streets (yellow poplar leaves carpet the ground), parks, woody ravines and deep gorges where the water runs fast. An unusually situated medina, divided by a gorge, decorated by trees and woods, which the Moroccans respect. "A cool oasis," the town is described as in the Guide Bleu. According to the name of the town, the river must run sulphur or saffron yellow at times. This is the site of an ancient Jewish community—Berber Jews. The wealth and reserved nature of the souk are evidence to this. Another strange, Moroccan/French town fifteen miles from Fez.

Samuel Beckett, I'm told, has a house here.

One must not judge these northern Moroccan towns in winter, when they are darkened by rain and sadness. I can easily imagine spring breezes rippling these poplars, and a quantity of sunshine illuminating the overgrown ravines. The outdoor, cane-walled cafés in full swing, and the sound of the river, fed by the never-dry sources in the mountains above, cooling the hot summer nights.

Now a sort of sodden purity pervades. Buying a pair of

yellow rubber boots, EA entertained a crowd of drenched children.

December 5 - Erfoud

This morning I woke up feeling guilty over my failure to finish this book. Then I looked over at my adorable wife. She knows how to make me happy. With her I've never been happier. At her side guilt amounts to an indulgence.

She's a remarkably flexible and resourceful young woman. How she makes me laugh! She touches me in so many places. That irresistible smile. Her sweetness and vulnerability gloss a complex personality.

Right now she's buried under layers of blankets and burnooses to keep warm in this fleabag N. African hotel. A fluffy woolen hat with a fringe makes her look like an Eskimo dozing in my bed. That's all she's wearing. A cuddly Eskimo nymphet with her skins off.

December 6 - Tinerhir

We decided to skip the sand dunes at Merzouga and come directly to Rissani for the market. Our trip was facilitated by Omar whom we picked up on the road. He informed us that:

• The market takes place Tuesday, Thursday and Sunday.

• It is a late market that does not get under way until noon so there's little point in arriving early.

• It is also a vegetable market where I should buy the desert onions that I relish for picnics.

• The gasoline is better in Rissani, the gas in Erfoud having been declared inferior.

In all this he was proved correct, confirming my opinion that the traveller does well to ally himself with Moroccans in these strange places. They are proud of their regional backgrounds and anxious to please. Omar went with us to buy a new djellaba. He owns a bit of land (barley, wheat, dates) in the palmeraie, reachable by bicycle. He is engaged to be married. He is young, poor and bored. He manages on charm and Moroccan reserve. But Ellen Ann didn't like him.

Beware of the desert types, he warned. They are shameless beggars.

In Rissani, I found camel-udder boxes in relative profusion. The jewelery ladies keep their wares in them. Ellen Ann bought a silver necklace and the black, colourfully decorated Saharan cloth. The Berber women fascinate her. Their flamboyant dress, flashing smiles and pretty faces, daintily tattooed, contrast strongly with the somber backdrop of the Sahara.

December 6

EA has just told me that each time she looked into the back seat Omar flashed at her. He had nothing on under his djellaba. No wonder she wanted me to get rid of him!

December 8 - Zagora

These desert mornings a coolness and tranquillity pervade the oasis. The stillness is broken by the twittering of birds and the thump of the farmer's hoe. One listens and listens; one gladly waits. A group of chattering children pass unseen on the other side of a mud wall. A donkey brays in the distance.

A breeze blows through here now, but when you're feeling sick, as I am, the gentle lift of air bears a cutting edge. One passes violently from shadow into sun. The sun is hot but, as the French say, the bottom of the air is cold.

Ellen Ann is having trouble adjusting to the Sahara. She thinks she's aboard another planet and feels uneasy in this alien land. A stretch of ugly black rocks between Ouarzazate and Agdz repelled her. They gleamed like oil

225

in the sun and dominated the spectral landscape—a vision of the world following the atomic holocaust. An unnerving sight. The first time I came here was in November 1965, having completed the first draft of *The Attempt*. I suffered from a bad case of strep throat. It was the date season, and the flies swarmed about. I remember thinking then, if I had had to look at one more black oily rock, gleaming in the sun, I would go mad. . . .

December 9

Another oasis morning. We open the window to let cool air and silence flow in. The earth, newly turned, smells fresh and virginal. Sparrows gobble up bread crumbs I have spread on the balcony railing. They squabble and knock some crumbs to the path below, where a cat waits. The cat gobbles up the fallen crumbs. Moroccan dogs love bread, but I never saw a cat eat breadcrumbs before.

December 11 - Ouarzazate

I feel ill, and this desert sun makes me shiver. Today at noon, in the market place of Zagora, I could feel the force of the sun striking right through the top of my skull, coursing like an electric current down my spine. I felt all right until I got out of the car; after five minutes in the sun I was ready to faint.

December 12

Ellen Ann envisions a chain of fast-food stores from one end of the Sahara to the other selling sunglasses and packaged ice.

She's just purchased some heavy Berber jewelry. Here she comes now, walking with a reassuring clank.

December 27 - Tanja

A Spanish woman walks past our door carrying a plastic

bag stuffed with yellow chicken feet. I say soup; EA imagines talismans.

December 29

I didn't sleep much, but awoke feeling relaxed and happy after a night in a warm bed. This Sunday noon we walked through the windy streets of Tangier to a restaurant for St. Pedro, cold white wine, strong coffee. Then back to our nest. I bought a *Trib* and laughed at all the comic strips.

December 31

Memories from the Sahara:

There will come a time when the West, exhausted from its insatiable thirst for material riches, will turn to countries like Morocco to re-learn the lessons of the spirit. The man lost in the desert who stumbles upon a green oasis where pure water flows. This is not a mirage.

ذِكْرَيَاتُ الصَّحْرَاء

سيَأتي يـوْمٌ حَيْثُ الغَرْبُ ، المُنْهَكُ بِتَعَطُّشِهِ الجَشِع إلى الدُّنْيوِيَّـاتِ، يُديرُ وَجْهَهُ نَحْوَ شُعُوبٍ كالمَغْرِب لِيتعلم الدُّروس الرُّوحِيةِ مِـنْ جَديـدـ: كالإنسَـان الضَّـائِعُ في الصحْـراءِ الـذي يَصِـلُ مُتعَثّراً إلى وَاحَـةٍ خَضْراءَ حَيْثُ المَـاءُ العَذْب مُنْسَابٌ. وهَذا لا يَعْني هُنَا السَّراب.

1978

January 18 - Tangier

Ellen Ann, David Herbert and I were lunching at Frank's Restaurant when EA spotted a man across the room who looked like Samuel Beckett. Only she had the nerve to approach his table and ask.

"Excuse me, but are you Samuel Beckett?"

His reply: "*Mais non, madame. Je ne suis pas Samuel Beckett.*"

"It's him all right," EA said, returning to our table. "Who else has a face like that?"

His brother, I'm told, owns a garage in Tangier.

January 27

This morning, having reached page 60 of novel (another mini-peak scaled), I went to be photographed for residence papers. The photographer's wooden stand-up camera, whose shutter was operated by hand, looked like a gadget Matthew Brady might have used. Then on to Dr. Anderson to have my sprained wrist X-rayed. His ancient apparatus belongs in a museum. An American doctor, when shown one of his X-rays remarked: "When was this photo taken—during the Civil War?"

February 19

This morning I saw wifette off on the 5AM bus to meet Muffie Amory who is in Rabat with her uncle, the Duke d'Uzès. So pretty she looked, an incongruously cheery presence among sleepy Moors in their hooded djellabas. Smiling and waving, full of love and anticipation as the bus rolled away into the dark.

March 1

Manu d'Uzès, the first duke of France, is in Tangier with his niece Muffie Amory. Raised in Bernardsville, N.J., he speaks perfect American English. He traded one of the most beautiful chateaux in France for amazing adventures all over the world. Now he lives in Rabat where he runs a diet clinic for rich dogs.

April 1

Betty Vreeland and Peter Tomkins, author of *The Secret Life of Plants*, are touring Morocco. When Betty lived in Rabat back in the '60s, she used to boss her diplomat husband around mercilessly. Now she gets told what to do by the macho and prickly Tomkins. Never seen her looking so pretty and happy.

May 14

Met Lilly Kalman's[1] poet/husband at her party. Prof. at Columbia. Dark, strange and emotional from years in the camps.

On to Paul's for one cigarette and tea. He peppered me with literary questions which meant he had begun reading the first chapters of *The Flight of the Pelican*.

May 23

In the vacant lot next door, the night watchman has invited whores for a party. A kerosene lantern illuminates the tent with alabaster effect. They are laughing and singing to the music of violin and drum. Every now and then a couple runs outside for a quick fling in the bushes.

---

1. Hungarian woman who owned a rug factory in the Kasbah.

229

Le Bal des Petits Lits Blancs was this year's major social splash. I resisted at first, thinking the tickets too expensive, but went in the end and was glad I did. Yves Vidal, proprietor of York Castle, spent months organizing the gala (half of whose proceeds go to the Cheshire Homes). Charles Sevigny, the American architect, arranged the decor with help from the Moroccan government. La Place de la Kasbah was commandeered for the occasion, and the Sultan of Morocco sent truckloads of carpets to be laid down on the cobbles.

A gigantic fire had been lit at Bab-el-Bhar to warm and welcome the guests as they arrived. The international set in fancy or formal dress were ogled like men from Mars by mobs of Kasbah kids kept at bay behind police barricades. Every few yards was a tented bar where champagne, Chivas Regal and Jack Daniels were served by white-gloved Moroccan waiters. La Place de la Kasbah, an area the size of a football field, was covered with hundreds of multi-coloured carpets. The effect was psychedelic, kaleidoscopic —an unforgettable sight.

Hassan II also provided musicians and dancers from mountain and desert all over his kingdom. The Kasbah reverberated with the sound of flutes, drums, ringing metal castanets and high-pitched chanting from swaying rows of bejewelled, tattooed girls in stupendous native costumes.

A Moorish feast was served beneath the arcades of the Antiquities Museum. Afterwards the dancing began in earnest and was accompanied by the ululations from Moroccan women who had swarmed onto the Portuguese ramparts to watch the show.

When we left, the sun was coming up, and the exhausted entertainers were bedding down on the carpets. One group of women from the Middle Atlas, dressed identically in gaudy green and gold costumes, slept in a circle, the head of one resting upon the hip of the next. They created a colourful woven rope not unlike the twisted silk cord that fastens my wife's Persian seed pearl necklace.

[John and Ellen Ann Hopkins spent the summer in London.]

September 21 - Paris, driving back to Morocco

Last night I was sitting at the Deux Magots signing a copy of *Les Mouches de Tanger* for Claude Thomas[1] and listening to a bearded individual strum a guitar. When he had done, he circulated among the tables, collecting coins. I gave him a franc which he accepted and passed to the next table. Suddenly, coins rained onto our table. The guitarist, with a crazed expression on his face, was hurling his money at us. As he went from one table to the next, he turned and threw the coins into our faces.

We got up and left feeling guilty, not knowing what we had done to earn the man's contempt. The man sitting beside us shamelessly pocketed all the coins within reach.

September 22

After a book signing at Gallimard, my editor, Michel Mohrt, took us to lunch at Le Voltaire. We were sitting on Montherlant's bench, discussing Graham Greene, when an elegantly dressed lady at the next table turned to us.

"Excuse me, but I'm Graham Greene's sister."

Mohrt, an ardent anglophile, immediately ordered more drinks.

October 1 - Sevilla

We're staying at the Doña Maria, a deluxe hotel with paper thin walls. A chorus of alarm clocks announces the

1. French translator of Paul Bowles; part-time resident of Tangier, she lives in Paris.

morning, along with the cranky twang of American female voices. The hotel is located opposite the Giralda, and an incessant clanking of bells makes sleep difficult after 5AM.

EA and I have gotten into the habit of recounting our dreams when we awake. We scream with laughter while flushing toilets roar around us.

This afternoon, on Calle Sierpes, the tiny son of a beggar woman, whose elaborate, wordy sign I could not decipher, came up and gave us the finger, hissing, "*¿Entiende?*" Over and over again. We laughed each time. "Psst!" The finger. "*¿Entiende?*"

Gypsies everywhere, displaying babies only weeks old. Apparently they have no shame; apparently they are indomitable. A vendor of nuts left his pushcart in our care while he went for change. He awarded us with a handful of tiny shrimp mixed with bugs.

Sevilla is plagued by rats. You see the anti-rat signs all over town. "Kill them! They eat our food! They're dirty! They eat the electric wires!"

We attended a picturesque but brutal bullfight this afternoon. The *rejoneador*, Domeq, managed to kill a bull from horseback; but what followed was butchery.

October 2 - Algeciras

Last night in Sevilla I was cursed by an aggressive gypsy woman in the street. "*¡Vas a morir en tu coche!*" she screamed. This morning we exorcised ourselves with candles and prayers in the Cathedral. EA draped a cross over the dashboard, gave me a St. Christopher medal to wear, and we arrived here safely.

October 3

Having heard my American accent, an elderly Englishman stopped me in the lobby of the Hotel Reina Cristina and launched into the wonders of the Panama Canal. "In Panama I found a thirsty tiger in a zoo, and made sure it was given water. And elephants, sir, must have salt! SALT!"

October 17 - The Parade Bar, Tangier

Abdelsalam, who told me the Panadero story I used in *The Flight of the Pelican*, had one too many:

"Juanito, tu eres muy correcto, alegre, todo conjunto como una bomba, con conciencia tranquila. Te amo demasiado, como un tatoo en mi pecho. Tu eres muy duro, un diamante entre dos peidras."

October 28 - طنجــة

Troubles:

My father has just undergone abdominal surgery. The tumour was malignant, but the doctor is confident he got it all out. EA's favourite relation, Aunt Mae, 97 years old, was found on the floor, unconscious after a minor stroke. She is now in a nursing home, where she cannot last long.

We are trying to produce a baby. If Ellen Ann gets pregnant we are going to say adios to Morocco and raise our family elsewhere. I feel I've been out of the mainstream too long and need to be near an English publishing center, which means either New York or London. Right now. I'm trying to finish *The Flight of the Pelican*. We go to the beach every afternoon to swim, lie in the sun and calm our battered nerves. The insomnia has persisted for two or more weeks now. We go to bed early, but rarely sleep before 4 or 5AM. The clock ticks as we toss and turn, sigh and think and worry, read and drink milk, take aspirin and sleepers.

November 2

Ernst Mayr, the Harvard evolutionist, in *Scientific American*, September '78:

"Once I gave a lump of sugar to a raccoon in a zoo. He ran with it to his water basin and washed it vigorously until there was nothing left. No complex system should be taken apart to the extent that nothing of significance remains."

November 7

Jean Genet is in town, staying in the Minzah. A balding, gnomelike figure chatting with his friends at the Café de Paris. Paul says he wants to see only Moroccans.

November 20 - The Marbella Club

Spain: where the children dress as adults; where children carry about children as big as themselves; where the children stay up all night.

I've been here a week now, working on the novel. Every morning I discuss the work in progress with Ellen Ann for three or four hours. Like the Lowrys, we make a good literary team. We sleep a great deal, sometimes ten or eleven hours a night. To compensate for the luxury (so far worth every penny, in terms of work accomplished and peace of mind) of staying at this expensive club, we lunch and dine in the cheap tapa bars in town. Sometimes we go to Puerto Banus, promenade along the quay, and try to decide which yacht will be Ben Bradshaw's. Yesterday, we bussed to the *refugio* above Ojen and walked back. About four hours. Today the leg muscles are tight. There's a heated pool, and we swim every day, sometimes three times. Dozens of laps. We see all the films in English, but mostly we talk about the novel. The character of Marie grows, fills out, and involves everyone in her sexual manipulations.

December 11

"The only possible redemption from the predicament of

irreversibility—of being unable to undo what one has done—is the faculty of forgiving."

—Hannah Arendt

December 28 - Tangier

Ellen Ann deliberated for days over what to serve for Christmas dinner—Turkey? Goose? Leg of lamb?—and finally settled on ham, which she would prepare from an old Arkansas recipe. I ordered the meat by phone from the pork butcher in the Zoco. What awaited me was not the fat red ham of my imagination but a long, lean haunch complete with hair and hoof. When I walked in with the thing over my shoulder, EA screamed, "What is it for God's sake?" She called her friends, and the majority reckoned that I had bought a "leg of pork." Recipe books were consulted all over Tangier. It was recommended not to remove hair, hide or hoof, but to roast and baste liberally with beer. The leg was so long the hoof stuck out the oven door. It cooked for several hours with many bottles of Heineken poured over it. The crackling, with hair singed off, came away as one huge shell. Beneath was the snow-white meat. Even M'rabet, who normally recoils in horror at the thought of eating pork, couldn't resist a nibble.

December 29

Boul de Breteuil, Marguerite McBey, Paul Bowles, David Herbert—all these long-time residents are utterly dependant on their Moroccan servants. With them they are able to lead comfortable, creative lives; without them they might all be in nursing homes somewhere.

December 30

Paul's birthday. M'rabet is throwing a party. He's having the Jilala in.

1979

I have come here for a change from Tangier, to refresh myself, and to work on the novel in a different setting.

This afternoon we ran into Ted Joans.[1] Not only beat but upbeat. God, how his artichoke and pistachio stories made us laugh! He has the only house in Timbuktoo with a telephone. The camel drivers drop by and talk on it incessantly; it doesn't matter that the thing was disconnected years ago.

And . . . Ellen Ann is expecting a baby in September!

Dr. Lucia Bedarida told us the good news. In 1965, when I was down with typhoid fever and Asian flu at the Italian Hospital, she saved my life with a dose of chloramphenicol. Now she claps her hands with delight at the sight of our radiant faces.

January 25

It's the rainy season, and *angulas* are in. The Spanish cook them in miniature clay casseroles with olive oil, garlic and red pepper, and eat them with wooden forks (the slippery little devils will slip off a metal one) as soon as the oil stops bubbling. They spawn in the mud along the banks of the rivers of western Spain and Morocco and migrate all the way to the Sargasso Sea.

January 26

The rain never stops, but we are comfortably ensconced

---

1. Itinerant American poet who frequently visits Morocco; author of *Black Pow Wow.*

236

in a large corner room at the Reina Cristina, with a hexagonal cupola balcony overlooking the sea. Every day I work on *The Flight of the Pelican* from ten until three and usually get so much accomplished that I proceed to get half drunk on Cuba Libres in the bar. Feeling triumph and relief we proceed to town for a late lunch of *gambas pil pil*, wild asparagus and *sopa de mariscos*. Gibraltar, where we were married a year and a half ago, is a soft grey mountain across the water. . . .

January 27

The rickety shutters of this old hotel have become unfastened by the wind and slam through the night. Will this rain never stop? Last night Ellen Ann came down with severe stomach cramps, and we wound up in the hospital down the street.

How I went through 4000 pesetas yesterday.

1000 lunch
500 doctor
500 provisions (booze)
400 medicine
300 dinner
1200 taxis
3900 + tips   (Not incl a 600 pta. rip-off by gypsy cab driver when I was frantically looking for a pharmacy in the middle of the night)

January 28 - Ronda, Hotel Reina Victoria

Today we took a train up here through the green hills of Andalucia. Spring has come howling into southern Spain, and after days of torrential rain and frightening winds, we were greeted by sun and a profusion of wild flowers. Fat pigs snoozed contentedly beneath the cork oaks, and we passed the diminutive, immaculately white Spanish RR stations one after another. Now we are living and working in this austere but comfortable hotel. A thick, icy wind moans out of nowhere as screeching eagles dive over the cliff. Rilke stayed here during the winter of 1912-13. His sad effigy surveys the valley from the garden. The *Duino Elegies*: once I knew them by heart.

January 29

Brrr! A chilly drizzle blurs the view. From my warm window I see Rilke's statue peering over the valley that cannot have changed much from the time of his visit (exactly 66 years ago today according to the hotel register). Last night the stars were out in force, and the voice of the river was clearly audible. Rilke teeters on the edge of the chasm, a lonely figure contemplating suicide.

January 30

Every time I look out the window I see a man standing in the garden, staring over the edge of the cliff. Rilke's gray eminence continues to spook me. Whoever arranged its placement there was not lacking in morbid imagination. This afternoon I walked the long valley beneath the town. Falcons darting, dwarf irises pushing up and water running everywhere. Mud and fresh spring air. My cheeks are gray-red and burning.

February 12 - Tangier

Anne Frank:
"It's really a wonder that I haven't dropped all my ideals. . . . Yet I keep them, because in spite of everything I still believe that people are really good at heart. I see the world gradually being turned back into a wilderness, I hear the ever-approaching thunder, which will destroy us too. I can feel the suffering of millions and yet, if I look up into the heavens, I think that it will all come right . . . that peace and tranquillity will return again. In the meantime,

I must uphold my ideals, for perhaps the time will come when I shall be able to carry them out."

The equanimity of children in crisis.

March 3 - Marbella

We have come back to Spain to collect Elizabeth David who flew in from London.

Scenes from along the road:

A pretty blond girl has taken off her shoes and sits bare-foot in the ditch, crying hysterically.

Another girl, older but no wiser, huddles beneath a blanket on the beach. The blanket heaves as she sobs her heart out.

March 5 - Tangier

Ellen Ann's chum Elizabeth David, the food writer, is staying with us. (Her ex-husband seems to have owned a restaurant in Tangier at one time.) She and Paul hit it off immediately. She's writing a book on bread and was eager to learn how the Moroccans make theirs, A-Z. Paul's helpmate Abdelouahaid Boulaich obligingly drove her to the countryside where Moroccan women in their colourful costumes harvest wheat with sickles. Then to the threshing floor where the animals go round and round. Then to the watermill where the huge stone pulverizes the grain. Abdelouahaid then took Elizabeth to his home so she could watch his mother prepare the loaf. Then to the local oven while it is baked. A perfectionist and notoriously difficult to please, Elizabeth returned thoroughly satisfied. She's fascinated by my description of sand bread, but the desert is far away. . . .

March 16

The man who can't find a match at midnight. He's afraid to go out because the streets are dangerous. Anyone who asks for a match after dark risks being mistaken for a thief and beaten up. The denouement: desperate for a smoke he finally does go out. When asked for a match, the terrified passerby compulsively empties his pockets. Our anti-hero goes home rich.

March 18 - Marrakesh

This city is overcrowded, with legions of artisans producing a mass of handmade goods. Coconuts piled on the Djemaa el Fna are a sign that trade with West Africa is up. The wind carried the dust as I packed up a few remaining possessions "thrown like hay" by the mad doctor from my house at Dar Tounsi. My desert days are over; the long Moroccan sojourn is coming to an end.

March 21 - Villa Taylor, Marrakesh

I lay awake at 5AM listening to the call of the muezzin. He speaks to me, too. Seventeen years in North Africa. Morocco has been good, but now it is enough. A little sadness is outweighed by exultation to be on the road again.

March 22 - مراكش

The Countess de Breteuil's seamstress who has undergone a mastectomy uses her false breast as a pincushion.

March 25 - Tangier

Noel Mostert, author of *Supership*, has become a recluse. No telephone, no car, he lives behind high walls and sees only Moroccans. You have to pound on the metal door with a brick to make yourself heard above the baying of the hounds. Once *los perros* have been locked away, however, no host is more welcoming than Noel. Honouring me with a glass of spring water from his well, he wants to hear all my news. Why doesn't he see anybody? I ask.

Not even Bowles?

He admits to having fought with all his neighbours.

March 27

Every morning dapper old Alec Waugh, in a broad Caribbean straw and Harry Truman shirt, steps into the noonday sun and walks a mile for his daily "communion" with a dry martini at Madame Porte's. Fernando the barman, who learned his trade at the Palace Hotel in Madrid, serves his icy *chef d'œuvre* in a pale green goblet around whose stem curls a delicate yellow tail, gouged, with some mysterious instrument, from the rind of a lemon.

We came upon Alec, toiling up rue de Belgique and gave him a lift home. He told me he once wrote twenty-six novels in twenty-six years. Now his siesta lasts, Tangier style, until the cocktail hour.

March 28

The best things in Tangier happen at 6 o'clock. At 6AM I drive to Cape Spartel for a swim in the Atlantic and a walk on the deserted beach; each evening at six we go to Paul's, sit at the master's feet, talk and laugh.

M'rabet: "Every year we get older, uglier and poorer, but look at Paul. Every day he gets younger, richer and better looking. What's his secret?"

Aeschylus in *Agamemnon*: "To learn is to be young, however old."

March 29

Tomorrow we fly away. The three of us—me, Ellen Ann and the babe inside.

Adios, Tanja.

Adieu, Marrakesh.

مع السلام المغرب

EPILOGUE

Deciding on England as the happy medium between Tangier and the U.S., Ellen Ann and I moved to London where our three children were born. We now live in Oxfordshire, in a National Trust house reserved for an American writer.

I used to think I had stayed too long in Morocco; that I had spent too much time travelling and not enough hours at my desk. Now I have come to look back upon those years as the most intensely creative period in my life. Tangier in the 1960s and 1970s was a paradise for a young writer. Polyglot and cosmopolitan, it teemed with colourful characters of every nationality; yet the city was small enough that I soon came into contact with the unique concentration of artists and writers who lived there.

We go back every year to visit friends. These diaries remind me how I miss the zany lifestyle, the warm weather and Mediterranean diet of Tangier. Many of the old residents have died, their beautiful homes are closed, but one vital ingredient remains: the ever-tolerant and welcoming Moroccans whose friendship, religion and culture make Tangier the amazing place it still is. I still dream of crossing the desert again. The boys say they want to come with me. In his book *Yallah* Paul Bowles speaks of the people who live out there:

> "How much ... we could learn from them about man's relationship to the cosmos, about his conscious connection with his own soul ... where we could learn *why*, we try to teach them the all-important *how*, so that they may become as rootless and futile and materialistic as we are."

☙

This
first English
language edition
of *The Tangier Diaries,
1962-1979*, printed for Cadmus
Editions, San Francisco, and Arcadia Books,
Ltd., London, by Cushing-Malloy in November,
1997 consists of a trade edition in wrappers; and for
Cadmus Editions, 76 signed copies in boards, 50
numbered and 26 lettered. Composed
and set in Linotype-Hell AG
Guardi by John Taylor-
Convery. Design
by Jeffrey
Miller.

☙